Sort It Out!

How to increase focus and become more organised in your small business

By Sarah Rugg

Sort It Out

How to increase focus and become more organised in your small business

First published in 2015

Published by Sarah Rugg.

ISBN 978-0-9931507-0-8

Acknowledgements

Thanks to my good friend Ali Finch for patiently listening to my crazy ideas and sharing my excitement. And my business partner Noel for holding me to account.

CONTENTS

"That's been one of my mantras - focus and simplicity. Simple can be harder than complex: You have to work hard to get your thinking clean to make it simple. But it's worth it in the end because once you get there, you can move mountains"
Steve Jobs

Introduction

"I don't have enough hours in the day... I could do with an extra hour... I don't have enough time... Where does time go...? "

No matter how much time you were given you still wouldn't have enough hours in the day. Face it: you'll never get everything ticked off your To-Do list. Once you accept this and stop beating yourself up about what you *haven't* done, you can move on and channel the precious time you do have into becoming more productive and enhancing your quality of life.

You see, it's all about changing the way you think. As long as you live you won't get everything done. The time we have is the time we have. So by accepting this and by digging deep to find what's important to you, your choices will become wiser and more radical, freeing you to move forward and embrace a new and refreshing way of working. You can put a stop to the busy-ness that isn't contributing to your overall goals. You *can* be more in control of your time.

Born out of my passion - or arguably my obsession - for getting organised, over the past 20 years I've studied people who constantly seem on top of everything and who get things done effortlessly. People who are never late, don't forget birthdays, arrive at meetings fully prepared, confidently decline engagements without justification, and never seem to run their phone battery or fuel tank low. They remain calm and unflustered in any situation. Nothing is a problem. And they always have time for a chat.

On a mission to comprehend how anyone could possibly be that organised and in control, I've followed these people, quizzed them, stalked them, learnt from them and adopted their ideas. I've read just about every time management book and blog going that relates to time saving or getting organised – or anything loosely linked to the topic. I've followed people on social media, soaking up the smallest of organisational or time-saving tips like a sponge. I became a little obsessed if I'm honest, looking for the elixir of time.

And, my conclusion was surprising.

These people are *not* naturally organised. In fact many of them previously led chaotic lives. They have simply implemented effective and well-thought-through strategies to deal with everything that is thrown at them. They have absolute clarity of vision and what's important to them is perpetually the focal point in their life.

I was seduced by this uncomplicated and minimalist way of life. The freedom. The simplicity. The precision of goals, objectives, ambitions. The laser-like focus on what's important.

I pledged to become *one of them*.

And with life being busier than ever - emails, phone calls, requests, social media and distractions coming at us from every angle - my mission extended to a search for the most efficient tools for streamlining a working day. And, it's still on-going. I researched extensively with fellow entrepreneurs and SMEs. I picked their brains about systems and software they use, I kept my ears to the ground about anything and everything that makes life easier.

I want to share my discoveries with you and challenge you to implement them. I'll take you through ways to save time and become more focused in your working day. I'll give you practical tips and advice that will transform the way you work and take your business to the next level. I'll show you how to create clarity and say no to everything and anything that does not contribute to your purpose.

I hope you'll find it rewarding and I think you'll be surprised at how easy a few simple changes are to implement and what a huge impact they will have on your working week. When you implement these strategies, it will open the doors to a flow of creative energy and inspiration. The blockages that were holding you back will be removed. So watch out, this is fair warning: you'll be on fire! Are you ready to accept the challenge?

Let's Get Started

The first thing you need to do is set aside a whole day when you won't be interrupted. If you work from home, consider going somewhere you won't be distracted by the household scene.

You will need:

- An open mind
- A willingness to become more organised and focused
- A commitment to implement the steps I suggest
- Your computer or tablet
- A relaxing environment

You will not need:

- Your emails open
- Your phone switched on

My virtual PA company - Vi-VA – will take your calls for a day. We'll also check your emails if you'd like us to. Why? So you can relax, enjoy the book and use the precious uninterrupted time to implement the strategies I suggest. It's a win-win. You'll reap huge rewards in your business as a result of doing this, and who knows, when you need a Virtual PA, you may just give Vi-VA a call. Just email hello@vi-va.co.uk to arrange it, with Sort It Out! in the email heading.

So now's the time to stop being a busy fool, reassess your priorities, implement some changes and say hello to a no-nonsense, highly focused and rewarding working schedule.

"Well, don't stand there staring. Best foot forward. Spit spot!"

Mary Poppins

"People often say that motivation doesn't last. Well, neither does bathing. That's why we recommend it daily"
Zig Ziglar

CHAPTER 1
Start with the Basics

Becoming a highly organised and focused business owner is not just about implementing practical tips. It requires a lot more than this. It's about attitude, modifying your lifestyle and embracing change. If you're 'on the bus' with this, then sit back and enjoy the ride.

If you're desperate to get to the practical elements you can implement from this book to become more organised, we will come to these. We'll cover systems you need to put in place, specific software and apps to use, filing tips, and lots more. We even go so far as to give you scripts to speedily dismiss unwanted sales calls. So before we launch into that, bear with me for this first chapter of housekeeping as it will make a key contribution to the bigger picture of becoming more organised and focused. It underpins the strategy, will bring clarity and help you to remain calm amid the chaos whilst maintaining your focus on what is truly important.

Define your Roles

If you haven't read **First Things First** by Stephen Covey you would really benefit from it. A thought-provoking time management book that makes you search inside yourself to find your true passion and drive.

There are some key points and practical elements from the book that you can implement now. These will keep you focused and make you think twice about accepting any tasks, meetings or invitations that are not in line with your principles and goals.

First, identify your roles in life. These are the bigger picture roles you want to play that are important, they should define who you want to be and where you want to go. Some of your roles may be necessary, rather than preferable, but most should be your choice.

For example, mine are:

1. Wife & Mum
2. Friend & Family Member
3. Marketing Director
4. Customer Service Director
5. Admin & Finance Director
6. Home Manager
7. Health & Wellness Manager

You'll notice that I've used the word Director a lot. Not because I want to feel important. This deliberate use of the word 'Director' psychologically implies that I am responsible. The buck stops with me. Seeing yourself as a Marketing Director is very different to seeing your role as just 'Marketing'. This subtle alteration of words is the difference between taking sole responsibility for growing your business and dabbling in some marketing when you have time.

OK, next, categorise or colour-code your online calendar – use a different category or colour for each role. My calendar has 7 colours. You can easily do this on most major online calendars such as Google calendar and Outlook.

Then, categorise each item on your To-Do list into one of your roles.

If any meeting, appointment or task doesn't fit easily into one of your roles, then you've got to ask yourself: Why am I doing this? How does it fit into my overall principles and goals? And if it doesn't, don't do it! 'Not easy', you say? I'll show you how you can make these decisions comfortably and confidently.

Let's use the coming two weeks as a test. Every time you are invited to a meeting, business lunch or networking group, asked to carry out a task, or invited on a night out, ask yourself the same question: Is this in line with my goals? If the answer is no, politely decline. It may take some getting used to and may even seem ruthless at times, but it is liberating and necessary for the new you. Once you practice it a few times, you'll find yourself implementing the strategy without thinking. That's when you'll know your attitude is shifting.

Health and Exercise

I've collated some high level tips on how to enhance your productivity levels. I'm far from a saint, I have to admit that I don't practice all of these all of the time, but when I do I see a marked improvement in my productivity. So, here goes.

To have the edge you need for making effective business decisions, you need to be alert. Obvious I know, but drinking alcohol during the week doesn't put you in the best state for the following day. There's only so long you can survive on late nights with a glass of wine or three to relax and shots of caffeine the following morning to recover from it. Eventually, you'll burn out. By all means have fun at the weekend, but try to avoid drinking Sunday to Thursday - a groggy business owner is *not* a productive one.

You'll benefit by drinking plenty of water every day. Dehydration slows your metabolism and results in fatigue, whereas staying hydrated promotes mental clarity for problem solving and enhances short-term memory. It's a no brainer.

Try to avoid foods high in sugar as they will give you a boost but this is soon followed by a real dip. Healthy snacks stabilize blood sugar levels. Nuts, seeds and dried fruit are good options to keep in your desk or bag as snacks.

As you'll know, exercise makes you feel energised. Brisk walking is great exercise as the combo of exercise and fresh air stimulates blood flow to the brain, and you re-gain clarity and focus.

It's not great to sit down all day. Make sure you regularly wander around and keep your body moving. Whether that's a good stretch or a walk around the block a couple of times, try to introduce movement to your day as a habit. The other benefit to taking a break, some light exercise or fresh air is that it can give you a fresh perspective on a challenge that's had you baffled.

Sleep

One of the main reasons for procrastination is tiredness. The average person needs between 7 and 8 hours sleep a night. Do you get that?

I thought not!

Work out what time you would like to get up in the morning then set yourself a bedtime by working backwards. For example, if you would like to get up at 6:30am and you need 7.5 hours sleep, you need to be going to sleep by 11pm. If you factor in half an hour for getting ready for bed and perhaps some reading, then 10:30pm is your new bedtime. Stick to it.

As a natural night owl, I was dragged kicking and screaming and with much trepidation into this alien routine. But I've now adapted and I'm reaping the benefits.

But before you set your new bedtime, I challenge you to get up one hour earlier than you do now. And before you night owls point-blank dismiss this concept, try it out - I am a convert. There's something invigorating about being awake at the crack of dawn and experiencing the tranquillity before the hustle and bustle of the day begins. It can be a perfect time for uninterrupted creativity and reflection. It may take a few weeks to change but once you get into the habit, you'll notice a positive difference.

If you're not a morning person, then you are likely to be a snooze-button addict. By repeatedly hitting the snooze-button, not only are you delaying the inevitable, but this futile attempt at getting more sleep is counterproductive. Not to mention torturous.

According to sleep researchers, a night's sleep is divided into five continually shifting stages, defined by types of brain waves that reflect either lighter or deeper sleep. Toward morning, there is an increase in rapid eye movement, or REM sleep, when the muscles are relaxed and dreaming occurs, and recent memories may be consolidated in the brain. The experts say that hitting a snooze alarm over and over again to wake up is not the best way to feel rested. 'The restorative value of rest is diminished, especially when the increments are short,' says psychologist Edward Stepanski, PhD who has studied sleep fragmentation at the Rush University Medical Center in Chicago. This on and off again effect of dozing and waking causes shifts in the brain-wave patterns. Sleep-deprived snooze-button addicts are likely to shorten their quota of REM sleep, impairing their mental functioning during the day. (New York Times, October 12, 2004).

Consider replacing your high-pitched intrusive alarm clock with a dawn simulator. Inspired by nature's sunrise, the increasing natural light wakes you gradually by sending a signal to your body to ease production of sleep hormones and increase those that help you get up and go. They claim to boost mood, energy and productivity levels.

So what else can you do to make sure you get a good night's sleep?

Follow the usual advice from the experts such as not eating late, not having high quantities of caffeine and minimising noise, light and excessive hot and cold temperatures where you sleep.

And, find a way to wind down just before you go to sleep. Especially if you absolutely *have* to work late (which you should avoid at all costs), your active mind may prevent you from relaxing. Try reading a book that doesn't require too much thought. I'd recommend avoiding self-development books that require actions or a large amount of concentration. Save these for the daytime.

I couldn't tell you in detail what the book I've been reading for the last few weeks is about. I know that it's a mildly amusing, easy read about a young mother and her day-to-day life. Perfect for the job - it lets me wind down, distracts my mind from the 100mph whirlwind that it's been going at all day, doesn't provoke any strong emotions and doesn't require me to do anything. The perfect remedy to switch my brain off. What winds you down?

And checking Facebook or playing games on your tablet is a no no if you want to get a good night's sleep! There have been a number of studies devoted to the potential disruption to sleep if using a tablet before bedtime. Many studies insist that looking at any back-lit device up to 2 hours before sleeping will suppress the natural, sleep-inducing hormone melatonin, and affect sleeping patterns. If you aren't getting proper sleep, you will wake in the morning not feeling rested and experience lethargic moments throughout the day.

Daily Implementation Time

It can be easy to find yourself at the end of the day not having achieved what you had planned due to constant interruptions. We'll tackle how to deal with these interruptions in chapter 9, but even if you rigorously follow the advice in this book, there will still be curve balls thrown at you - challenges that you can't anticipate.

This is why it's important that you assign around 90 minutes each day to focus on the growth of your business. If you don't, your business development will always play second fiddle to interruptions. It will stagnate. Or worse still, your profits will decline.

Your 90 minutes should be rigidly scheduled daily, preferably first thing in the morning. The hour you will gain from rising earlier is the perfect time. If you add an extra 30 minutes to this, you're done and dusted before the disruptions ensue.

I call this 'daily implementation time' deliberately. Not strategy or marketing, as this would suggest planning and tactics. The key word here is implementation. The importance of this is crucial. You can have amazing ideas until the cows come home but if you don't execute them, what's the point? Implementation is what separates the achievers from the fantasists.

Ninety minutes is a guide. You may choose to adapt this to suit your working day. But I'd avoid doing more than 90 minutes, as this pushes over into potential procrastination territory and makes it into a bigger job than it needs to be. And preferably don't do less than 45 minutes - this is the most important task of your day, so give it the time it deserves. Remember, this is the main driver for your business growth. During this time do absolutely nothing else. Be unreachable. This is a prime time where the phone needs to be off, the internet disconnected and emails closed. If you have an office close your door.

OK, so what to do in this magic 90 minutes?

This will vary largely for every business, so to give you an idea, I'm talking implementation of marketing campaigns, writing blog posts, writing copy for your auto-responders and mailings, sending e-newsletters, creating new offers or packages, selling them on social media... anything and everything that will contribute to the growth of your business. So pledge to do something in this time *every single day* to grow your business. Remember, these 90 minutes are when you are working *on* your business, not *in* it.

Be mindful that the tasks carried out during this time need to be in line with you goals. It's purely a way of making sure that your marketing strategy actually happens. Working in a structured manner and in line with your marketing plan will make sure that you get the most out of this hugely productive time.

If this sounds a little overwhelming, don't worry. You'll learn the knack of breaking tasks down into achievable bite-sized chunks further on.

If you can force yourself to do this every single working day, it will become habitual and a way of life. You will be in control of your day and feel empowered and motivated to embrace it. No matter what interruptions occur, you can rest assured that you have contributed to your business growth.

Put down the Tablet

We're a nation increasingly addicted to electronic devices. So when you've finished your day's work you may find yourself sitting there all night with your tablet, watching TV, and dipping in and out of email, websites, Twitter, Facebook or whatever.

Use of tablets specifically has become an obsession. So much so that larger companies with sizeable advertising budgets are choosing to invest that budget in online advertising, in place of traditional TV commercials. This is largely due to the tablet-on-the-knee-whilst-watching-TV culture. The tablet gets significantly more of our attention than the TV commercials do.

OD-ing on technology will affect your productivity for tomorrow. Give yourself a clean break if you can in the evenings from tablets, computers, and gadgets. Not only to give your eyes a rest but to regenerate.

Try to spend time doing something relaxing even if it's just watching TV – without your tablet on your knee!

Start each day on a positive note

Express gratitude. Before you even get out of bed each day, remind yourself of 3 reasons why you are fortunate. This might be your children's health, a partner's love, your warm bed. It could be use of your sight so that you can observe natural beauty – rainbows, sunsets, flowers. Or perhaps the good food and wine that you enjoy.

Although some may think this sounds a little 'woo-woo', this approach is a powerful and positive start to the day, which will quickly influence your mindset and mood.

Surround yourself with positive, like-minded people

It's empowering to be utterly intolerant of pessimism.

Pessimism is a time-sapper, not to mention an energy-sapper. It's contagious, and easy to be drawn into by other people if you're not disciplined in your approach to it. Negative emotions reduce the brain's capacity to think openly and find creative solutions.

Can you think of someone you know who approaches everything with a 'why it *can't* be done' mentality? A 'half-empty' person. Think about the last time you were with them. How did they affect your mood? How did you feel after spending time with them?

Now think of someone you know who is positive-minded. A person whose glass is half full. Someone who doesn't see anything as a problem: *"Not to worry, we'll get around that"*... *"You've lost client X? That must be a relief to you, you'll have lots of time freed up now to find another less demanding client"*... You get the gist. How do you feel after spending time with them?

Which of these two people would you rather spend more time with?

Searching for reasons why you *can't* do something is the biggest waste of time I have ever come across. You'll never get that time back.

It's our natural tendency to dwell on negative thoughts and magnify them. Remember that you control your own thoughts, and they can be powerful. Look at negatives as a positive: *What did I learn from that situation?* Perhaps you just lost a client. That may have been a good thing. Seriously. Everything happens for a reason. If you look hard enough you'll find that reason. And if you can't find it now, it will become apparent in the future.

Using positive phrases and always looking for the solution to every problem and the silver lining of every cloud feels good. Aim to become an eternal optimist. 'There's no such word as can't' is a phrase that was drummed into me from an early age. Simple but powerful – it *makes* you find a way to overcome challenges.

As this often doesn't come naturally, it will take time and effort, but it can change your level of motivation and drive tenfold. There is no doubt that you are significantly more productive when you're in a positive state of mind. The world is your oyster.

A 'can do' attitude is powerful. A force to be reckoned with.

Visualise yourself as a highly successful achiever. Live every moment as if you are that person and it will only be a matter of time until you get there. Having this attitude will radiate positivity which ultimately means that you will get more done.

Find Clarity

Until you have clarity for your purpose, your vision, and your goals then it's an uphill struggle trying to increase your productivity. Managing your time and staying focused day-to-day requires a high level of clarity in order to know what to say no to and what to prioritise. As I mentioned at the beginning of this chapter, reading (or re-reading) Stephen Covey's *First Things First* is a great place to start to help with this.

Once you are clear on your vision you need to picture it and live it. Try visualisation. Andy Murray, Jessica Ennis-Hill and Muhammad Ali are amongst many successful people who use (or have used) visualisation as a method to achieve their goals.

Practicing affirmation is also powerful. Use this with any of your goals (try to keep to a minimum of three), but to start with, let's focus on the reason you're reading this book. Tell yourself repeatedly 'I am highly focused and efficient'. You don't have to say this out loud. By repeating positive affirmations several times a day, you are training your brain to believe them and after a while you'll start to internalise them.

What would it look, feel & sound like for you to be more organised, more focused and to have a healthy work/life balance whilst still running a highly successful business? Visualisation and affirmation are a powerful combination. Don't underestimate what you can achieve through using them.

It's a good idea to set intentions throughout the day in everything you do. Link these to your goals and vision. Aside from keeping meetings and tasks relevant and on track, it's a good reminder to question whether everything is in line with your goals.

Brene Brown, a research professor, author and speaker, is endorsed by Oprah Winfrey. Here's why she thinks you should set intentions:

For me, setting intentions is a power move. It's how I bring clarity, meaning and purpose to my day, my meetings, a conference call and even daily conversations. Setting intentions helps you get clear on why you're doing something (clarity), why

it's important to you (meaning) and how it moves you closer to your values (purpose).
      ~ Brene Brown~

Find your Perfect Coach

I fully recommend working with a coach or mentor. Apart from it being a wise thing to do, they will make sure you get things done. They will push you, challenge you, and provide invaluable support for your business and for your personal growth. They will instil the discipline necessary to achieve your goals, providing encouragement and helping you hone your skills along the way. You'll benefit from a balanced, honest and objective viewpoint, which, with all good intention, you may not get from friends or family.

Small business coaches are generally entrepreneurial characters, who fully understand the issues experienced by small business owners, as they've been there themselves – or they *are* there themselves. Experienced coaches will provide wisdom and insights to springboard your business.

Some tips for selecting the right business coach or mentor:

- Talk to them first. There has to be chemistry. A good coach will offer a free consultation and will only work with you if they feel that there is chemistry. The same goes for you – you should only work with a coach whom you 'click' with, after all you will be spending quite a bit of time with them.
- Check out their experience – how long have they been a coach for? What size of businesses do they work with? Are they a business owner themselves? What is their background?
- Do they have testimonials? Look at their LinkedIn profile and the recommendations on there.

- Choose someone who regularly invests in his or her own development. Someone who stays up to date with what's happening both in the business world and the bigger world. The benefit you get from this is invaluable – you are kept up to date with cutting edge information about business growth and trends.
- Decide exactly *what* you need help with – is it general growth of your business, or something more specific such as franchising or marketing.
- Consider whether you would rather have face-to-face, telephone or Skype coaching sessions. You may not have the choice with all coaches, but it's something to consider when asking questions and researching.
- Listen to recommendations. If someone you trust recommends a coach or mentor to you, just as if they had recommended a good plumber, definitely consider them.
- Be clear on cost and whether your coach is available between sessions if need be – ask if that is included in the price, and if it is, use it.

I can personally recommend Gavin Preston, a business mentor who has made a huge difference to my business and my personal development. His genuine passion for helping business owners is contagious. I have quoted Gavin below as it explains, much better than I could, about what Gavin is about. All I can say is that I wholeheartedly agree and endorse it:

I love what I do. I love the moment when the 'penny drops' with one of my clients, when there is a flash across the eyes of one of the business leaders I work with; when all of a sudden 'all becomes clear', when I help them realise what has been holding them back and what they can do to change things. I love seeing the wider impact across the companies and businesses I work in and the results that follow.

I 'hold up the mirror' to my clients and know when to provide robust challenge and when to support. An effective, although not always comfortable process.

I consistently 'up' my own game, investing each year in my own professional and personal development and learning the latest strategies. I seek to spend time around like minded successful people who, as a group, inspire and support each other to step up.

I am on the journey myself and now share my insights, strategies and techniques with my clients to help them achieve the business, career and personal results that they want. I care about the people I work with and take the attitude of "do whatever it takes to get the result".

Who is your perfect mentor? Take the necessary steps to find him or her today.

If you implement the advice in this book, you will become more focused, efficient and aware of how the day-to-day clutter fits - or doesn't fit - into your overall purpose. It will give you a solid footing and a kick-start to increased profitability in your business. Combine that with working with a coach and you'll be flying.

Clear your Mind

It's always recommended that you keep a pen and paper by the bed so if you wake in the night remembering something you have to do, or with a brilliant idea, you can simply write it down and go back to sleep without it playing on your mind.

There is nothing different about those same moments in waking hours.

If you have anything running around inside your head that is taking up thinking space, you need to remove it. Until you clear your mind, you won't be able to move forward and execute the strategies that I am going to take you through.

So, please take a few minutes to write down (or make notes on your phone or tablet if you prefer) any tasks that are stressing you out, *that are not already on your To-Do list.* In other words, things on your radar, but in your head only. These don't all necessarily have to be tasks – they can include decisions you need to make (what to do with a contractor who isn't performing, which school to send your child to, best invoicing system to use, and so on).

Ok, now take the piece of paper and put it out of sight, somewhere where you won't lose it. Or, close the Notes on your device (for now).

Now you can stop worrying about those tasks for the time being. They are captured and will be dealt with by your new super-slick system that will be in place before you've finished this book.

Right, we've now got clear headspace and we're ready to move on.

Self Acceptance

Until you accept and embrace yourself - warts and all – your judgment and decision-making can be clouded.

Self acceptance gives you the confidence to execute tasks with precision and clarity and to say no to people. It allows you to be sure of your own decision-making ability, and to believe in the decisions you make. Yes, you can trust your own judgment.

It all saves time. How? Quicker decisions mean no wasted time um-ing and ah-ing or sitting on the fence. You say 'no' with such conviction that people don't try to persuade you otherwise. They accept your answer the first time.

Not only that, but it gives your clients (and your team, if you work with one) confidence in your ability. An under-confident business owner will naturally generate a higher number of questions from clients and potential clients who are looking to seek assurance that you can do the job proficiently. It all takes up your time and can be avoided.

'Accept myself? - That's a big ask coming from such a small section in the chapter', I hear you say. Yes it is. And clearly it's not something that's going to happen overnight. But I want to sow the seed, and point out how it can contribute to a more productive – and of course happier – life. So, let's cut to the chase - how do you self-accept? Well, I'm no psychologist but I can give you a few tips that may help. Some food for thought:

- Write down your strengths. Every single one of them. No need to do anything with the list - it's simply reinforcement to yourself
- Forgive yourself for past regrets – that may be wishing you had gone to Uni, making a social faux pas, making a certain decision in your business. You can't change the past, so tell yourself that you did what you thought was best at the time. And move on from it
- Look at who you spend time with. Does anyone speak to you negatively? Who encourages you and who doesn't? Who believes in you? Maybe it's time to distance yourself from people who you identify as having a negative impact on your self esteem
- Don't beat yourself up. Internal negativity is damaging. We *should* make mistakes, otherwise how do we learn? As long as the mistakes aren't continually repeated.

When you find yourself metaphorically beating yourself up, ask yourself: *Would I say that to a friend or relative if they were in my situation and I was talking to them?*

Frame of Mind

What frame of mind are you in? How much energy do you have at the moment? What are you capable of? What are you not capable of? What will you fly through? What are you not in the mood to do?

Learn to gauge your own state of mind and what you are capable of.

If you've not had a great night's sleep or if you've been drinking last night (on a school night? tut tut, slap your wrists), you may struggle to concentrate on tasks such as working on your accounts. Or you may be in a particularly chatty mood so now may be the time to make those phone calls that need doing today.

Don't be scared off that you have to stick to a rigid regime. Be self-aware, live in the moment and manage your time according to what you are capable of at that moment.

The only exception to this rule is your Daily Implementation Time - that should be the only real rigidity in your day's schedule.

Step Away from Perfectionism

There's an important difference between having high standards and being a perfectionist. Yes, high standards should come as a benchmark in business. But perfectionism is a time-consuming, unhealthy pursuit of excellence. Perfectionists are intolerant of mistakes, prone to fear of disapproval and can experience decreased productivity. It certainly takes its toll, and can seriously distract you from what matters most in your business.

A healthy achiever on the other hand takes genuine pleasure in trying to meet high standards. They generally lead a more stress-free existence.

Be ruthless! Do you really need to do that? Are you making a difference? Will a lesser job suffice? Ask yourself is your effort disproportionate to the value of the task? What else are you jeopardizing by exercising perfectionism on this task?

Go on, I dare you to do a less than perfect job.

Take Time Off

You're no good to anyone when you're burnt out. Not yourself, your team, your clients. And certainly not to your family. You become inefficient, caught up in a downward spiral of habitually working long hours.

Stop! Now! Have a word with yourself. Take yourself off and chill for the rest of the day.

You are achieving less by working long hours when you're fatigued than if you were working shorter hours when you're refreshed. It's not rocket science. You tire yourself out and as a result become less productive and don't function as well. Tasks take you more time to do as you're less focused. It's as simple as that.

You're also likely to be neglecting your family and friends. So remind yourself why you are running your business, and what's important. Keep that balance in the forefront of your mind.

Try to re-energise by taking at least one day off every week, perhaps a Saturday or a Sunday. Preferably both (although, I do live in the real world and understand that 2 days off is rarely possible when running a business).

Make sure you take a regular holiday. Whether that's a fortnight in the Seychelles, a long weekend camping in Bognor Regis or some time at home with the family - just do it. It can be energising to know you have time off booked - some downtime to look forward to.

If you follow the strategies in this book, you'll find that you have extra time in your day, so you shouldn't need to work late anyway.

Have Set Working Hours

Aside from the fact that working from home indefinitely impacts on your personal life, not having set working hours can mean that you meander through a day with no fixed end point. This can negatively impact on your concentration.

When you work from home make sure you define your working hours, as if you were employed by someone. Be strict in sticking to them.

If you know you categorically finish at 5pm, you will generally work a lot more efficiently than if you don't have a defined finish time. And the beauty is that in the hour leading up to 5pm, you work a lot harder and faster than if you didn't have that boundary in place. Without it, you may well work on into the evening, and that's when you start to become inefficient and burnt out. It can become habitual and it is a slippery slope. There is nothing more effective to focus the mind on completion as a deadline – in this case the deadline is your finish time.

Consider setting a reminder alarm to go off one hour before you finish so that you are even more aware of this.

A few years ago, my work day usually ended with a comment from hubby as he walked through the door (looking around disapprovingly), which translated into 'What on earth have you been doing all day?'

Grrr.

However, since being more explicit with my working hours (Rome wasn't built in a day, it took a bit of educating him), he now understands that during the daytime I'm not a housekeeper, neither am I a laundry or errand-running service. Once that was clarified, everyone knew where they stood and my productivity soared.

When you've finished work, switch your computer off and move your paperwork out of sight. Don't work until tomorrow. Be very disciplined with this. Communicate to everyone you live with and to your friends what your working hours are and be firm on those boundaries.

Take Regular Breaks

As if you were in employment, think about what breaks you are going to take and roughly when. Then allow yourself to take these breaks and enjoy them. You need them more than ever in your own business when everything is reliant upon you. You need to be in good shape mentally to make smart decisions, to take swift action and to do this with a level head. You need to be on the ball. Remember, the buck stops with you.

If you need to book a doctor's appointment, catch up with a friend, pop into town or to the supermarket, it's a good idea to get into the habit of doing it in your lunch hour, just as you would in an employed job. If you apply this discipline, you'll enjoy a more structured working life.

Don't get me wrong here, I'm not suggesting that you tie yourself to a completely inflexible schedule. Of course the main benefit of being self-employed is the flexibility. If your child has a school assembly that you want to go to, the only doctor's appointment available is smack bang in the middle of the morning, you need to let off steam by a visit to the gym or ease your aching shoulders by booking in for a massage, the beauty is that you can choose.

Applying the discipline of regular breaks is more of a guideline. It's about getting into a habit of segregating your work life from your personal life, and it will prevent burnout.

If you work at a computer, make sure you take regular short breaks throughout the day. Go for a walk - round the house or office building, in the garden, whatever, but just get up and move around. As well as the health benefits of taking a break from a computer screen, you will work more productively after each break. You'll feel refreshed and have higher concentration levels.

If you don't excel at it, Outsource it!

My wise friend and colleague John, a psychologist and executive business coach, firmly believes that it is much more effective to exploit and maximize strengths than to focus on improving weaknesses.

He says: *"This came from my commercial training experience where most companies used performance management to highlight areas of weaknesses and then send people on courses to try and improve them. Weaknesses can be improved but the problem is they will never become a strength, the best you can do is aim at making them closer to the average. World class performance comes from finding the areas where people are already good or excellent and developing these strengths to make them superlative. That's how Olympic gold medallists are selected and coached."*

You probably already know your weaknesses in your business. Be honest with yourself, write them down. Then identify your team's strengths. Assign tasks to team members who will excel at them. Don't waste time and effort trying to teach people how to do something that doesn't come to them naturally. If you maximise the abilities within your team, then the rest... outsource those tasks to an external expert.

Not only will this save you stress and time, but it will actually save you money. If you think about it, by handing over those tasks that you dread every month, and quite frankly are not very good at, you'll have more time to plough into what you're great at, and your work will be more rewarding and enjoyable. And a bonus - these tasks will be done to a high standard, probably in half the time it would have taken you. Ch-ching! Remember, you didn't start your own business to dread the work.

Compose Yourself

Consistently exude calmness and control. Be the person who takes the reins in a situation, diffuses panic and provides reassurance. If you portray a calm demeanour, a person in control of whatever is thrown at them, you are much more likely to become that person.

Skidding sideways into a meeting with *"Sorry I'm late"*, telling people how scatty you are or how bad your memory is could be damaging to your own reputation and that of your business.

Whether you like it or not and whether it's a conscious consideration or not, people will judge you on how you act. They will see your behaviour as a direct reflection of your business and how it is run. Tardiness in you is not appealing to someone who is looking to use your company to carry out time-bound work, for example. They need reliability. Just as turning up to a business meeting or event looking shoddy can lead people to believe that the work you deliver will be the same. Be aware that you are the face and the characteristics of your business.

If you ever feel yourself getting upset or annoyed, simply say, "We'll discuss this later/tomorrow," and walk away. Don't waste time and energy at that point. Things will seem clearer later, and even more so the following day, if it will wait that long.

Once you finish this book, you will be more in control. You will have organisational systems to capture everything and, more importantly, to filter out paraphernalia that isn't part of your overall goals and your purpose on this planet.

"Less is more"
Robert Browning

CHAPTER 2
Your Work Environment

OK so you're now on the road to being mentally prepared. Next, let's tackle your work environment.

Working Environment

It has been proven that there is a direct correlation between workplace design and business performance.

An effective work environment should provide positive sensory stimulation through colour, lighting, aroma, space and furnishings. The temperature is important too. And let's not forget noise levels.

Whether you are conscious of it or not, these elements all affect your performance. When you get them right, it can enhance productivity and creativity, and can even affect how you respond to change.

Poor workplace design, by contrast, is linked to lower business performance and higher levels of stress.

Look around you. How does your work environment make you feel? Is it clutter free? Are there distractions around you? Notice the lighting, the scent, the temperature, the sound. Are you as comfortable as you might be? Is this a place where you can find inspiration? Does it feel 'right'? Is it a calm place where you feel at ease?

Look at what could be changed to make it your own inspiration station. And make those changes happen.

Remove Distractions

Firstly you need to identify and remove any distractions from your work setting.

When I started to work from home, each day would involve me dipping in and out of tidying up, doing the occasional wash load, answering personal calls and plenty more non work-related activities. Not great for productivity.

If you find yourself being distracted, take action to prevent this behaviour. If you don't have a home office and have to work in a lived-in room of the house, it helps to have a whirlwind tidy in the evening, leaving your work environment clear for tomorrow. It means you don't need to spend any of your valuable working day looking at a mess or, worse still, tidying it up.

If you work in an office, the same applies. Look at what your distractions are and remove them. If you find yourself drooling over your Rosie Huntington-Whitley calendar or your Bradley Cooper screensaver, consider replacing it with a motivational quote that is meaningful to you or a Vision Board (also known as a Dream Board). Not as attractive perhaps, but more inspirational.

Your Immediate Workspace

This should be clear. Only have visible what you need to do today (and don't be unrealistic about your To-Do list – see Chapter 4). All other work should be out of sight.

Is the positioning of your immediate workspace logical? Do you have space to write / review hardcopy information? Is your shredder, printer and bin to hand?

Are the key pieces of stationery you use regularly within reach – stapler, post-its, etc? Same question for envelopes, stamps, cheque book (yep, some people still write cheques), paying in book, online banking keypad. Do you have a good supply of printer paper? Plenty of pens? Spare A4 pads?

I suggest you buy a 5 drawer desktop filing cabinet. You can get these from most stationery stores and online too. They come in all designs – from faux leather to brightly-coloured... plastic to metal. They can actually look good as well as being functional.

These filing drawers can house all of this necessary but unsightly paraphernalia, keeping it out of sight. Remember, your aim is to clear the decks of distractions.

A suggestion is to use them as follows:

Drawer 1:   Pens, stapler & staples, post-it notes, etc.

Drawer 2:   Envelopes & stamps

Drawer 3:   Reference material (brochures, items to access for future reference)

Drawer 4:   For 'someday' filing (paperwork you don't need to do anything with now, but you may want to refer to at a later date)

Drawer 5:   Paper for printer

And don't bother with a fax machine. Who uses fax nowadays? It's just another potential interruption. And it's ugly. An unnecessary distraction and time-waster when it goes wrong. So get it on Freecycle or eBay and let's move into this century.

Set up an Organiser File

This is *not* a filing system. We'll cover filing systems for retaining paperwork that may (or may not) need to be accessed in the future. But the majority of paperwork knocking around on your desk is probably just outstanding tasks waiting to be actioned. So, we need a system for keeping this under control.

I can highly recommend an organiser file for this – a simple but brilliant invention that I've been using for years. A system that can keep the most disorganised of us organised.

Take a few moments to think of the most common things that you receive paperwork for. I suggest you have a quick flick through your in-tray – this should give you the answer. Remember, we're only talking about *hardcopy* stuff here, not emails or electronic files.

Next, grab yourself an organiser file. At the time of writing this, you can buy them via my website: vi-va.co.uk/getorganised.

If you're wondering what organiser files are, they are robust portable divider files. A great way to organise paperwork to hand (but out-of-sight) to be dealt with imminently. There are usually 12 sections. Here's a suggestion for sections I find work well:

1. Goals	It's important to put these at the front. You should review them regularly
2. To-Do Today	This should be cleared at the end of each day. It's dedicated to more urgent or important stuff that needs to be done as soon as. The only paperwork in here should directly relate to an item on your To-Do list *for today*
3. To-Do – Non Urgent	This is for paperwork relating to items on your To-Do list but not for today. Never put anything in this section that is not on your To-Do list, as it is likely to be forgotten
4. Team	Matters you need to speak to your team or contractors about is kept here. Each time you speak to one of your contractors/team, check in here.

	Similarly, if there is anything you ask your team to do you could jot it down and put it in here so it doesn't fall off your radar
5. Pending (or waiting for response)	This is for paperwork that's been dealt with as far as you can and you are now waiting on someone or something. All items in here should be on your To-Do list for follow up
6. Inspiration	As a business owner, some days can be lonely. Invest a little time in collating your favourite quotes, pearls of wisdom - whatever motivates you. Refer to it when you are struggling to get motivated
7. Strategy	This is a good place to stuff ideas into that relate to strategic planning for your business – competitor's flyers, notes, articles, etc.
8. For Meetings & Appts	Paperwork that relates to meetings or appointments in the future should be kept here. How many times have you had a meeting and not been able to find the agenda or forgotten a confirmation letter for an appointment?
9. Finance	Throw receipts, statements and any other paperwork relating to your accounts into here as you go along. Once a month, pass it on to your bookkeeper (or accountant). Remember to write on the receipt what it was for BEFORE you put it in the file

10. Reference Information	Sometimes there is information that you want to keep and refer to occasionally. In this section I have samples from our printing company, price lists, book recommendations and keyboard shortcuts
11. Client Information	Useful to use for information relating to *active* client work only. It means you can access it quickly and easily for all current client projects
12. Other	You can use this for whatever suits you and your business. For mine it is Strategy information for my other business

You may want to replace or change some sections. It has to work with *your* business, but the above will give you a good start.

The beauty of this system is that you can instantly and effortlessly access information relating to your current projects, clients, finances, etc. I refer to mine constantly. It is also portable so is remarkably convenient if you, like me, work in more than one location.

Have you noticed that the sections of this organiser file are for business related items only? Don't be tempted to mix sections for your personal life with your business life. The concept can be repeated for personal / family life. However, it's important to keep them separate.

Go! Implement. See you shortly.

Become Paperless

If you're not already paperless, then you would benefit from introducing a new online way of filing. More about online filing in chapter 7, but for now we need to tackle your existing paperwork.

First, try to file as little paper as possible. Yes, not very technical or ground-breaking advice, granted.

Secondly, consider taking a photograph of or scanning a document, then saving it online. Then bin it.

Thirdly, if you are a Gmail user, there is absolutely no need to print and file emails – you can access any email quickly and easily (even if it is archived). Think of Gmail as your new filing system. More about Gmail and its benefits in Chapter 5.

If you prefer reading hardcopies of emails, this is purely a habit that you can get yourself out of. You are duplicating work and it's neither productive nor environmentally friendly.

If you absolutely *have* to file a physical item, file it in your very simple filing system (see next section).

Right, now let's tackle the paper mountain that has accumulated from *before* you implemented the above.

OK, so assuming you do have a pile of paperwork (or 'In Tray' contents or whatever you want to call it). Put it in front of you on your desk. Tackle it one piece of paper at a time, with the goal being to reduce it to zero. Don't cherry pick, just work down the pile in order. Once you pick it up, don't put it back!

Be ruthless in your questioning and assertive in your actions when sorting through this pile. Does it still require your attention? Often you'll find that it's been completed by someone else or it's no longer relevant or it's too late (you've missed a deadline). C'est la vie! In the bin.

How long has it been there? If it's something that's been there for a long time, does it really need to be done? Just because a business colleague said it was great for his business to register on here doesn't mean it's going to be great for yours. How much value is it going to add to your business? Is it going to stay sat there for another few weeks unattended to? Can you give it to a team member or your Virtual Assistant to action? If not, bin it.

Stay mindful of your overall goals. If it doesn't contribute to them, bin it. If it does, do it now if it will only take a few minutes. Otherwise, delegate it or add it to your To-Do list. Now that it's on your To-Do list, can you bin the hardcopy paperwork? If not, add it to the 'To-Do non-urgent' section of your organiser file.

I'm a real note-taker, but I'm also a minimalist. I scrawl on paper for all sorts of reasons. I don't like these bits of paper lying about everywhere, but I can't bring myself to get rid of them – 'just in case'. If this resonates with you, I've found a solution that works perfectly and it's simple - transfer everything from your scribbled notes that needs action onto your To-Do list, then throw your notes into a box or filing drawer. This is your comfort blanket and can be accessed when need be (you probably won't access it 95% of the time, but for that 5% when you may, it's there).

For anything that doesn't fit neatly into the To-Do list category, consider using an App such as Evernote to keep a record of it. You can use it to note recommended software that you may want to try at some point in the future, a fantastic hotel that you must stay at sometime, gift ideas, books to read, your Bucket List! If you take the time now to set up some categories in an app on your tablet, phone or laptop, then when something interesting comes onto your radar, you can quickly add it to the proper category – making it so much easier to refer to in the future.

At the end of this go-paperless exercise, your shredder will no doubt need emptying, but your desk should be completely clear with nothing but your computer, phone, notepad and pen.

How good does that feel?

Find a Filing System that Works for You

The next step is to find a filing system that works for you – somewhere to house the paper you absolutely have to file.

It took me 15 years of beautifully coloured and labelled lever arch files sitting empty on a shelf next to an unruly mountain of paperwork to realise that I wasn't the kind of girl who would neatly hole-punch and file paperwork in this way.

Then came along my wonderful desktop filing drawer units. I now own them in every shape, size and colour. I use them for both business and personal. I toss papers in the relevant drawer and there's not a hole-puncher in sight. My lever arches are long gone and I don't miss them one bit. My filing is painless.

If you do have a volume of paperwork and it's absolutely unavoidable, filing drawers may not be the answer for you. A concertina file may be more beneficial. You can get one to sort paperwork by month (January to December), by day (1st to 31st) or alphabetically (A to Z). They are easy to file in and easy to access paperwork from.

The point is, unless you have a PA on site, you need to choose a *realistic* filing system to keep your paperwork under control.

If you think your paperwork is too big for either of the above solutions and we're getting into the realms of hardcore tall metal filing cabinets, you need to be asking yourself some serious questions about why it is necessary to keep this level of paperwork. Is it something you've always done? If you can't definitively give a reason why you keep this paperwork, it's time to change. How often do you actually refer back to it? Do you have enough space? What if you had a fire? Could it be online instead? Is it you or your system that is the dinosaur here?

Every 6 months have a purge of your filing. And be ruthless. Add a bi-annual recurring To-Do item on your list for purging paperwork.

Basic Tools for Small Business Owners

Aside from the obvious computer, printer and shredder, below are some basic tools that any business owner would benefit from having:

ITEM	GREAT FOR...
An in-car phone charger	Those situations when your phone's battery is running low and you're on the road
Hands-free equipment	Taking and making calls whilst driving. Optimising the 'dead' time
A 'meeting folder' with A4 pad	Carrying everywhere - meetings, networking, etc.

Business Cards	Handing out at all opportunities. Always keep in the car, your wallet/purse and in your meeting folder
A Bungee Wallet	Keeping your own business cards together and intact.
Business Flyers	Handing out/leaving places at every opportunity. Always keep in the car and in your meeting folder
A spare main's phone charger	Those situations when your phone's battery is running low. Especially if you're away on business
Filing drawers	No-nonsense filing. I recommend either 'Bisley SOHO Multi Drawer Cabinets' or the faux leather equivalent (at the time of writing this Ryman sell them)
L-shaped A4 pockets	All sorts! Especially keeping paperwork together and segregating paperwork into tasks
A label printer (and spare tape)	Labelling anything and everything – filing drawers, A4 pockets, your cat. Anything. Very handy. (A basic mains-operated one by Dymo or Brother is sufficient)

"The art of being wise is the art of knowing what to overlook"
William James

CHAPTER 3
Managing Your Workload

I'm not saying it's easy, so this chapter will offer you tips on how to get the things done that *really* need doing. I'm talking about tasks that grow your bottom line, tasks that contribute to your overall goals. The important stuff.

Recognise Urgent vs. Important

	Urgent	Not Urgent
Important	**Quadrant I** Urgent and Important	**Quadrant II** Not Urgent and Important
Not Important	**Quadrant III** Urgent and Not Important	**Quadrant IV** Not Urgent and Not Important

In his book *The 7 Habits of Highly Effective People*, Stephen Covey famously explains effective personal management through use of a quadrant.

Quadrant I is for the immediate and important deadlines.

Quadrant II is for the longer-term strategising and development.

Quadrant III is for the pressured distractions. They are not really important, but someone wants it now.

Quadrant IV is for those activities that yield little value. These are activities that are often used for taking a break for time pressured and important activities.

Urgent tasks require immediate attention. They're usually visible, right in front of you; often popular with others and fun to do. Important tasks are generally more tedious; however they achieve results, and contribute to your mission, values and goals.

Your time can be consumed with reacting to urgent tasks, leaving the important tasks neglected. The problem with dealing with urgent tasks constantly is that it is a stressful existence. You're constantly working towards looming deadlines, you're under pressure, the quality isn't as good and the reliability isn't as strong.

Set aside time to focus on non-urgent important tasks. By doing this the volume of urgent tasks will naturally reduce and your business will become more effective and profitable in the long term.

Streamline Your Workload

The most effective way to get through your workload is by grouping tasks.

If you keep switching between, say, dealing with emails and calling customers, you have to re-focus your mind for each task. It's much better to concentrate on one group of tasks, such as ploughing through your emails until they're all done, and then switching to making calls. You get into that 'mode' and as a result move swiftly through your 'To-Do' list.

Try dividing your 'To-Do' list into groups – have a section for each group, e.g. phone calls, emails, research and errands/out of office tasks. When you add a task, make sure it's assigned to the appropriate group. You can then sort them (assuming you have an online To-Do list) by group at the click of a button.

Save tasks in the 'email' group for the allocated time when you are checking your emails anyway (covered in Chapter 5).

When you have an errand to run – something to drop off, pick up, etc, think ahead. Look at your calendar - when are you likely to be passing near that place. If you can kill two birds with one stone, this is a much more effective use of your time than making single trips out.

Just Say No

Stand your ground and don't be afraid to say no.

Never apologise for saying no if something is not in line with your goals. Don't be a box ticker. Question everything: Do I really need to be doing this? Is this in line with my goals? If it's not the best use of your time or contributing to your purpose, then, as we said in the opening chapter of this book, don't do it.

To get used to saying No on a regular basis, practice it in the mirror – just for kicks. It feels great! Be polite with it of course. Say it with a smile. Offer an alternative date or option, or some helpful information, for example: "I won't be able to do it, but Claire has the skills you need for that job, you could try her" or "I'm really pushed this week. If you go to thetrainline.com you'll be able to find that information on there" [smile sweetly].

Another response to use is *"I can do X for you and I can do Y. But I can't do both by [Date]. Which is the most important?"* This shows someone who is confident and in control of their workload.

Be bold. You can get away with all sorts if you say it with a smile. Say *No* to everyone you need to say no to - friends, family, colleagues, contractors, and customers.

Yes, even to customers. As you'll know, some customers will push boundaries if you let them. Make sure you agree firm timeframes and guidelines upfront to clearly set the expectations of your customers. Have them written into your T&Cs in plain language terms. Re-affirm them verbally or via email at the beginning of a new customer relationship. Don't be afraid to politely but assertively say 'no' if their request falls outside of those terms. If you feel that a customer is sapping your time and energy for little return, focus your energies elsewhere.

Keep it Real

Organisation means effective planning.

At the end of each day, plan for the next. But before you write your To-Do list, consider the meetings, appointments and calls that are already scheduled in. And the unplanned stuff too - is it typically a busy day of the week for you?

My To-Do list is consciously shorter on Mondays as it's our busiest day for enquiries through incoming emails and customer calls. Do you know your busiest days of the week?

Is your list achievable? Be honest with yourself.

Speak It

Think about dictating emails, reports, presentations, proposals, blogs, social media updates, manuals, updates to documents... anything that can be dictated saves you time. Dictation may not be for everyone, but you can train yourself to work like this over time.

You'll also need to get yourself a great Virtual Assistant with oodles of initiative (I believe Vi-VA are very good!) A good VA will fill in gaps, correct errors, and basically, just get on with it - with minimal interruption to you.

If you don't want to use a Dictaphone or don't have one, then you may want to try software such as Dropvox (nope, not a typo) – it's voice recording software that loads straight into your Dropbox account. How clever is that? Your VA can easily pick it up from there if need be.

And the great thing about dictating is that you can do it wherever you are – sat in traffic (on hands free of course) or waiting for an appointment. You can even walk down the street doing it - if you're dictating into an app on your phone, it just looks like you're having a phone conversation!

The Fudge Factor

Every day is different and brings surprises along with it.

You can make your day so much less stressful by applying the fudge factor to everything you do. When going to a meeting or appointment, leave 10 minutes earlier than you normally would. When planning your day or week, don't be naive and fill it to the brim convincing yourself that you'll get through it all. Because invariably you won't. Factor in fudge. This helps to deal with those unexpected tasks, phone calls, visits, traffic jams or anything else unplanned that you come across as part of everyday life.

And remember that being late to meet someone is rude. It shows disrespect for them and suggests that your time is much more important than theirs. Not true at all. It's basic manners; every human being deserves the respect of you being there when you say you will.

If you work with someone who is consistently late delivering, apart from questioning why they are still working with you, consider applying the fudge factor into the deadlines you give them. If the work is due on Thursday, tell them Tuesday. It makes your life simpler and saves some chasing time.

Unexpected Time

One of the great benefits of applying the fudge factor is that you regularly find yourself with unexpected time available.

Remember to make the best use of it. But remember to keep firmly focused on what's on your To-Do list, and nothing else.

For example, if you arrive early for school pick up and have 10 minutes sitting in the car, what is on your To-Do list that you can do now? Making a phone call perhaps? Sending a text? Reviewing what you have left to do today? Perhaps you can do some dictation. You can even use the extra time to give thought to how you are going to achieve one of your tasks.

If you are sat in a waiting room or reception area with a little time to spare, review a document or do some reading. As long as it's on your To-Do list, and is contributing to what you need to achieve by the end of today.

Later on when we get to checking emails, I recommend checking them no more than twice a day. However, there's nothing wrong with checking emails in your 'dead' time. Especially if you have an iPhone - there's something particularly satisfying about checking emails on Apple's Mail app on an iPhone. It's not quite the same on an iPad or a Mac – just the iPhone. Perhaps it's the therapeutic one-touch zap where each email disappears like a puff of smoke and the next appears as if by magic. You can swiftly move through your emails with a single touch for each one (Tip: If you do this, make sure the 'view' on your Mail is set to Gmail, so that all the spam has already been taken out).

It's always a good idea to carry the relevant materials with you wherever you go, such as your phone, the book you are reading and your organisation file. You're then prepared and will have everything you need to make the best of this welcome bonus time.

If this sounds too much like all work and no play, worry not. The harder you work during the day and the more you get done, the more play time you have after you clock off. *That's* your incentive to work zealously to get today's tasks completed.

Be Accountable

Daunting as it sounds, *you* are solely responsible for your own time management and getting things done. You can't rely on anyone else for this. Not your team, not your business partner, not your colleagues, not your family. *You* are responsible for making sure your time is managed in a way that means you can lead the life you want. It's important that you recognise and take this responsibility on board as it will change the way you function.

If you're delivering a product or a service to a client, make sure you tell the client when you'll have it to them by. And once that expectation is set... Never, Ever, Miss the deadline!

It's a good idea to have specific turnaround times outlined that you stick to unfailingly. Consistently adhering to these will become a habit and you'll start to do it without thinking too hard about it. These deadlines should be drummed into your team or extended team and form part of your contract with them.

If you're working on a non-client job, it's easy to persuade yourself that it can just wait another day. Treat every task as if it's for a client – don't move the goal posts, stick to the deadline you have set yourself.

Identifying a mini-mentor – perhaps someone close to you whom you trust – could be one of the best things you do for your business. It could be a partner, friend, family member - someone who understands you. Explain to them that you are going to work differently starting today; you need to be held accountable for completing tasks and you would like their help with it. Make sure you choose someone reliable, firm, and most importantly someone who strongly believes in your business (you'll find that a lot of people can be ruled out under that latter point unfortunately).

Or alternatively you may want to consider partnering with a like-minded business owner or entrepreneur. Even if your businesses are in totally different sectors, you could hold weekly updates via Skype for say, half an hour, to go through what you've achieved in the past week against plan and to say out loud your goals for the coming week. You hold each other accountable and it gives you that extra push to get things done. It's also a great opportunity to share ideas and thoughts.

If you work alone and from home, you'll know that this can be a lonely place at times. Connecting with someone in the same boat can be an effective and rewarding partnership.

The One-Touch Rule

The most productive and organised people I know actively apply a one-touch rule and adhere to it day in, day out. It's part of their daily life.

How often have you picked something up, had a quick look and thought I'll come back to that later? The same is true of reading an email, opening your post or listening to a voicemail and deciding to deal with them later.

When you pick something up but don't fully deal with it, it's still on your mind. It's obstructing your focus, even if you don't realise it. It's using up energy, which you need for the immediate task in hand.

So, the general rule is simple: if it can be dealt with within a couple of minutes, do it. If not, put it on your To-Do list. At this stage, don't give too much thought to *how* and *when* you will do it, just put it on there to clear your head. And if there is any paperwork relating to it, put it in your organisation file.

Eating Frogs

There's a huge benefit from eating your frog before you get started on the day's work.

If you're thinking 'crazy woman' and you have no idea what I'm talking about, then you should read Brian Tracy's *Eat That Frog* book. Here's a summary:

There's an old saying that if the first thing you do each morning is to eat a live frog, you'll have the satisfaction of knowing that it's probably the worst thing you'll do all day. Using 'eat that frog' as a metaphor for tackling the most challenging task of your day - the one you are most likely to procrastinate on, but also probably the one that can have the greatest positive impact on your life - Eat That Frog! shows you how to zero in on these critical tasks and organize your day.

OK, so now we're all on the same wavelength.

Have your frog as the highest priority on your To-Do list. Visualise yourself having done it and the feeling of relief and satisfaction that brings.

When you are in the shower in the morning, or walking the dog, or whatever you do that allows thinking time, take that one task from your To-Do list for today and plan how you are going to tackle it. Focus on absolutely nothing else apart from that task. Clear your mind of all other tasks for today. Give it your full attention. Remember you are not doing it, you are simply thinking about *how* you may do it.

Ask yourself what is stopping you from starting it. What's causing the block? What can you do to overcome this? (see Chapter 10) How can I chunk it down? Although after you have implemented the strategies in this book you shouldn't have large tasks on your To-Do list – only bite-sized chunks.

By channelling all of your thoughts into this one 'frog' of a task, even if only during a five-minute shower, you will find more clarity and you will be less daunted by it. Honestly. Try it.

One Thing at a Time

Multi-tasking is often unavoidable in day-to-day life. If you only have 30 minutes between picking your children up from after-school club and dropping them off at football training, then of course you can't singly cook a meal, make sure they're changed and washed, clean their football boots, search for the missing shin pad, break up a fight, and oversee homework in that time. You multi-task. And you make it. By the skin of your teeth, but you make it.

There are some choices of course. You could have said no to football in the first place. You could have prepared the meal beforehand or even driven by McDonalds on the way to football (gasp). You could have sent the kids with dirty faces and football boots. And so on.

The reality of it is that this type of scenario is part of daily life, especially if you have a family. In a work environment however, multi-tasking is just not productive.

If you are checking an email at the same time as being on a phone call, you are not giving the email or the phone call 100% of your focus. And there will be repercussions. The upshot is that you may miss something important or absently-mindedly delete an email. It will also be apparent that you're not paying attention. We've all been on the phone to someone when you know full well you haven't got their full attention – they pretend they heard what you've said, but you know they haven't by their vague - and sometimes strange – reply. There are odd silences and sometimes you can even hear the background typing. How rude!

There are numerous similar examples of how we multi-task in our businesses. If you are texting whilst on a Skype call then you're not paying attention. You may miss a key point, then be unexpectedly asked by the meeting chair: *'What are your thoughts on that, Sarah?'* D'oh!

Multi-tasking will almost always come back to haunt you at some stage and will be a vampire of your time. Here's how.

Take the above example of taking a call whilst checking emails. Let's say one of the emails you were (impolitely) reading at the time you were talking to your client was from a colleague. It was an invitation to a networking event. You didn't really read it properly – you absent-mindedly thought (whilst chatting to your client on the phone)- *another* networking event, I go to enough already, and I don't even like them. And you hit delete.

If that email had received your full attention you would have seen that the event was dripping with the type of clients your business is looking for. In fact, an entrepreneur that you've been trying to recruit as a client for almost a year now is on the attendee list. If only you had focused your full attention on that email.

In the meantime your client on the other end of the phone is quite frankly, a bit miffed. He pays for an attentive, professional service from you and didn't get it on this occasion. In fact, it's probably the third time now that sort of conversation has happened lately.

He's feeling unloved. Unimportant. Sure that he's not being listened to. And he's quite right. He's started to mention to a couple of colleagues of his that he may be looking for a new graphic designer as the one he has (you) seems to have gone off the boil a bit. He begins to surmise. Perhaps they've grown too quickly and are too busy? Perhaps they've lost interest? He doesn't really understand the reasons, but he knows he can't rely on a business that he is rapidly losing faith in.

These situations will come back to bite you on the backside. As well as costing you money, they are a vacuum of your time. The time and effort you have to put in to gain new clients is increased - you could have potentially had some handed on a plate to you at that networking event. But one of your competitors attended and got there first. Your client eventually will switch to another graphic designer, unless you get your act together pretty sharpish, change your ways and show them some love.

If you have the foresight to anticipate these consequences, then you will think twice about multi-tasking in the first place. And if losing existing clients and missing opportunities to find new ones isn't enough of an incentive for you to stop multi-tasking, consider this: apparently there is scientific evidence that multi-tasking is linked to short-term memory loss. Now you could do without that

Multi-tasking is like perfectionism. Its benefits are a myth. You are fighting a losing battle. The sooner you realise this, the more productive you will be.

Enjoy every task. Lose yourself in it. Enjoy the moment. Slow down. Focus on one thing at a time. Appreciate the satisfaction.

Death by Meeting

Meetings are often unnecessary time-wasters. A killer of your precious time. If you've worked for a large company, I don't need to tell you this. Small business owners do tend to be choosier about meetings as time is money. Their own money. But I still see meetings happen for meeting's sake. And it drives me nuts.

Is it Necessary?

Question every meeting. Does it really need to happen? Do you need to be there? Can it be done via Skype? If you *must* have a meeting, make sure you have an agenda – and stick to it.

The next time someone suggests a meeting, ask yourself:

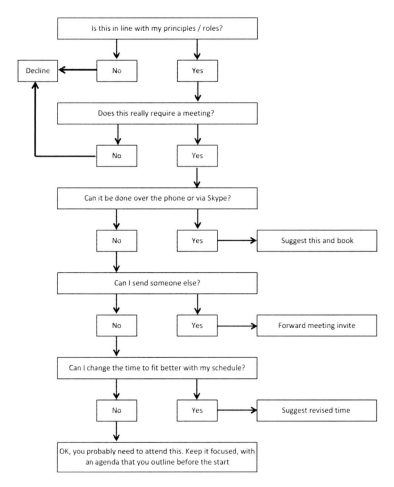

Holding an Effective Meeting

Preparation is everything.

Make sure you put a note in your To-Do list to prepare for the meeting in advance. Have a very specific agenda. This will avoid the *'Argh! I forgot about that meeting'* syndrome when it's suddenly upon you.

Set your stall out at the beginning of the meeting. Explain that you only have X amount of time and you need to be out of there by X time. Make sure you wear a watch so that you can check it indiscreetly at regular intervals during the meeting. Yes, I did just say *in*discreetly. You'll be surprised at how much more productive the meeting will be and it will ensure a prompt finish.

Every meeting should start by defining a specific outcome. For example: "the objective of this meeting is to come to a final decision on..."

...as opposed to:

"At today's meeting we will discuss... ". This is vague and doesn't define an outcome.

If you find that the meeting is unproductive, quickly try to get it back on track. If that fails, make your excuses and leave. If that means feigning a text from a colleague, do it. Ask to be copied on the minutes or follow up actions. That way you won't miss anything key. Life's too short to waste it on unproductive meetings.

Follow Up

If you happen to have called the meeting, I would say it's probably your responsibility to 'take minutes'. Assuming this isn't an official meeting that needs to be documented from start to finish (such as a legal or disciplinary meeting), I'd suggest you do a simple follow up email as follows:

> *Thank you for meeting up today. Please find assigned actions with deadlines:*
>
> *SJ to write 6 blog posts – due 15/3*

NG to draft proposal as per discussion – due 20/3

JG to communicate Feb 2014 changes to contract team – due 22/3

Please confirm to me via email when your action is complete.

Another option - even quicker than this – is to use a whiteboard during the meeting to make brief notes and to record actions. At the end of the meeting simply take a photo of it and email it out to everyone. You can even do it from your tablet or phone there and then. I do this all the time and it works a treat and saves a load of time on writing up minutes.

If it is your responsibility, or in your interest, to make sure the actions are followed through, add a follow-up task to your To-Do list. The quickest and easiest way to do this is to copy & paste into your To-Do list a link to the email you sent out with actions on (if you sent a photo make sure you include yourself on the email). Or alternatively add it onto your To-Do list there and then, referencing where the photo is saved.

Make your Life Easier

When booking a meeting in your calendar, if you don't know where you are going always it's useful and time-saving to include the address with postcode, or any directions that have been given.

Always ask if it is easy to find. I never cease to be amazed by people who don't even offer so much as a hint of assistance to find their office that is so obscurely situated that even a private detective would struggle to locate it. And of course you don't find this out until you are anxiously driving around just before your meeting is due to start. So avoid this situation by asking the question in the first place.

Another question to ask upfront is whether there is available parking. Once again, I'm surprised at how many people just leave it up to you to stumble upon the nearest car park whilst getting confused in a one-way system of a busy city.

It's a good idea to save the contact telephone number of the person you are meeting in your phone (or the number of reception there) - if you have no internet access and you are lost, you may need to call them.

Use Your Tablet

I would say it's perfectly acceptable in this day and age to take your tablet into a meeting. If you can be disciplined that is - and not use it to check emails or read social media during the meeting.

To save time on the day, you may want to call ahead to the meeting venue and find out the Wi-Fi network name and password. You can then use your tablet to take photos, recordings and notes.

The time I used to waste after meetings going through hand-written notes, struggling to decipher them, transferring them onto a To-Do list, liaising with a bunch of people to arrange a suitable time for a follow up meeting (which usually involved a chain of emails bouncing backwards and forwards for some time) was unnecessary.

Taking your tablet into the meeting – with Wi-Fi – means that you can put actions assigned to you straight onto your To-Do list (assuming they are in line with your goals of course). And if you are responsible for doing the minutes, you can type brief notes and actions straight onto an email as they arise.

If you need to book a follow-up meeting, book it in then and there using your online calendar – add the relevant people to the item on your calendar so they receive an invite into their inbox.

Hey presto – the meeting delegates have the 'minutes', actions and the follow up meeting confirmation in their inbox before they've even left the room.

As you walk away from that meeting, everything has been captured and nothing needs immediate action. You can conserve your energy and focus on the next task on your To-Do list for today.

Reading

You simply won't have time to read everything, so there is a genuine necessity for cherry-picking here.

To cut through the mass of business publications, online articles, emails and other reading, first scan the headers – is there anything of interest? If no, bin, delete or move on. If yes, read it there and then (assuming it's only a few minutes). With business magazines, limit yourself to reading only a couple of articles.

Ask yourself; can I delegate the reading to someone else? Someone who could whittle out the important or interesting information and summarise it for you.

Readers are Leaders. As a small business owner you'll know that your business - and you personally - will reap rewards as a result of reading relevant books. But where on earth do you find the time for this?

Take the book you are reading with you wherever you go. Have it in your folder, your car, handbag, wherever. Whether you are early at a meeting, waiting for your child to come out of an appointment or sat in the dentist waiting room, read a little. You'll be surprised at how quickly you get through it.

Download the e-version on to your tablet - so it's accessible to read wherever you are. Sometimes it's nice to have a hardcopy of a book, but in the interests of efficiency, we can't deny that e-books serve a great purpose.

If you have to read a lot of business books, you may want to consider booking yourself onto a speed-reading course – it really will pay off. Personally I like to lose myself in a book in my own time, to absorb it, re-read parts and make notes. Speed-reading does have its place, but don't let it impact your enjoyment.

Chasing People

It's frustrating having to chase people up in business and it shouldn't have to be like that. But unfortunately the reality is that due to various reasons – typically complacency, disorganisation or apathy – pursuing people for overdue actions is something you just have to do sometimes. These people are time sappers and are frankly inconsiderate and unprofessional.

The best thing you can do to minimise time spent chasing these unreliable people is avoid them like the plague in the first place. For people you work directly with, I would suggest some firm words need to be had. Having to chase them up is not good enough if they're going to be working with you. Try to get them into the habit of getting back to you about everything unfailingly and within the allocated timeframe. Otherwise they are out. It should be as simple as that. Very few people – arguably none - are indispensible to your business.

We entrepreneurs can be control freaks but for the sake of time and stress, place your trust in people you work with and empower them to deal with tasks – give them the benefit of the doubt. When you delegate to them, forget about it. Trust that they will deliver. If they have a history of not getting back to you, and it relates to an important task, for example, a customer request, then put a follow up on your To-Do list to make sure they do it. You may also want to ask yourself why they are still working for you.

For others outside of your team – clients themselves, suppliers, people whom you don't normally deal with regularly - always follow up. Put a quick note on your To-Do list (copy & paste a link from Gmail – if the task/information was requested by email), e.g. *'Chase Mike [copy & paste link]'* and add date. Then forget about it.

To get the best results, think carefully when asking people to do things for you in the first place. David Taylor, Leadership coach and author of The Naked Leader, believes that *'There are three words that are so powerful, their impact is awesome'.* Those words are: A person's name, 'would' and 'because'.

Notice the difference it makes by using people's names. It personalises your request and the recipient will assume greater responsibility for the task. Plus people generally love hearing their own name!

Use of the word 'would' is something I adopted after reading *The Naked Leader.* The results of changing just that one word have blown my mind. Here's David's explanation of why it works:

"Picture the scene. It's bedtime for your son or daughter. You say 'It's bedtime now, Michael, can you go to bed please?' Michael's subconscious thinks, 'Can I go to bed, am I physically capable of doing this? Yes, but I am watching TV at the moment, thank you very much...' or

'Rebecca will you tidy your bedroom?' Rebecca thinks, 'Will I, now she is asking me to predict the future, which I am unable to do...' or

'Claire, could you pick up that ice cream wrapper please?' Claire ponders, 'Could I, now he doubts my ability to...' etc. etc.

The word 'would' - to adults as well as children, is powerful because it gives over command of the position, ownership of the request, to the other person, in a way that does not in any way doubt their abilities. By the way, this is not political correctness gone mad, it is the way that we think as human beings..."

And finally 'because'. By using a brief explanation of *why* you need a particular task doing, it adds context and gains buy-in. People are more likely to complete a task for you and meet the deadline for it if they understand the reasoning behind both the task and the deadline.

By making these subtle changes you'll notice a more positive response. Anything to get things done!

Consequences of Choice

Remember every action that you take will potentially result in more work for you.

Every newsletter you sign up to will involve an inbox attack - useful or not, it will require extra reading and extra work. Most emails you send out will get a reply back into your inbox. Every item you purchase could go wrong and may need to be returned. Every voicemail you leave will potentially generate a returned incoming phone call. Every app you download will take time to learn. Every book you buy will need reading.

These are examples of everyday actions we take without giving thought to the potential consequences and impact on our time and our life. Each action dilutes the simplicity that we strive for.

So think about the outcome before you do something and question 'do I really need to do that'? Then ask yourself, 'is there an alternative'?

For example...

Signing up to e-newsletters:

1. What value will I get from receiving these emails?
2. Is it in line with my goals?
3. Realistically, am I going to have time to read them?
4. Am I just adding more pressure on myself?

5. Can I use my VA to receive them for me and pick out the ones I need to see?
6. Can I sign up to receive updates directly to my feed reader instead of my inbox?

If you decide after answering those questions honestly that you really *must* sign up, then set up a filter (or rule) on your email so the e-newsletter goes directly to a named subfolder. This way the email hasn't come in to your regular inbox, cluttering your day, and you can go to the relevant folder at a convenient time to read the newsletter.

Emails generate replies:

1. Do I really need to send this email?
2. Why do I need to send this email?
3. Is email the best form of communication?
4. What happens if the person doesn't reply and I have to chase them up?
5. Would a phone call be easier/quicker?
6. Can it be sent by text instead?
7. Am I speaking to that person later/soon and can ask/tell them then?

Voicemails breed voicemails:

1. Do I *really* need to speak to that person?
2. Can I text instead of calling?
3. Do I need a response from that person?
4. If not, and you are simply notifying them of something, text or email saying 'FYI only – no reply necessary'
5. How do I want that person to respond? If you'd prefer a text (say, you were on your way into a meeting), then state this.

Always be mindful that you create your own work. The more things you decide to do - whether that's re-vamping your website, redecorating your home or changing web hosts - the more work you are creating. So think twice about whether it is absolutely necessary and whether this is the right time to do it. Unless the items are genuinely pressing, try to do these things when you have a lull.

If you've put a day aside to do some thinking or strategy planning, or if it's a weekend or you're having a day off, just be aware that if you're sending emails the day before you will likely get replies the next day when you're not there to respond. Unless of course you take our advice and use a Virtual Assistant (see Chapter 8), in which case you don't need to worry about this as your emails will be checked and responded to for you.

Delegation

If you are someone who says *'It would be quicker/easier to do it myself'*, have you considered that *you* could be the problem and it could be your delegation skills that are at fault?

Be crystal clear with instructions. Don't expect someone to complete a task to your exact requirements if you don't give them enough to go on. Some make the mistake of telepathically communicating detail when delegating a task. In other words, assuming that everyone thinks in the same way as them and has the same standards and opinions as them.

It's well worth investing time upfront to express your preferences and expectations, and detail such as how you would like work returned to you, what systems or software to use, how you would like to receive any queries (email, text, phone, etc). It may be *'quicker to do it myself'* for the first couple of tasks but you will reap the rewards in the long term.

Try to refrain from stepping in to help. If you do this, you're not giving your PA / VA the opportunity to learn, and also it may be expected next time.

Be considerate. If possible, avoid sitting on work then suddenly delegating it as a last minute task. Not only is this unfair to the person you are delegating to, but it's bad management on your part. Landing it on someone without giving them sufficient time to think about it could result in more questions than usual in a short space of time, causing you to think *'it's easier to do it myself'*. Whereas if you'd have planned better, your PA / VA would have had more time to consider it and make informed decisions without having to increase the likelihood of error by rushing it.

Regularly ask your VA / PA how you can make delegating to them easier. By asking for this feedback, you will save time and money in the long term. You are also involving them in the business, making them feel more a part of it. There's a whole chapter on how to get the most out of a Virtual Assistant later in the book.

Random Thoughts

You need to reboot your brain, just as you do your computer. Clear your cache by brain-dumping your thoughts and ideas.

My nickname for quite some time was "RT" (short for 'Random Thought'). My mind jumps from one thing to the next like a flea with a sore backside.

As a business owner, and particularly as an entrepreneur, your brain is wired and your ideas free-flowing. They often come to you at the most unexpected moments. They are gold dust. You are brilliant. It's so important then that you have a system to capture these RTs. They may relate to a client of yours, your marketing, a new product idea, or anything else, ahem, *random!*

I'd suggest that you keep things simple and just quickly add them to your To-Do list as and when you have these light bulb moments. This way they remain on your radar but out of your head space.

Taking all of the thoughts out of your head and putting them on paper (or straight onto your To-Do list or an app such as Evernote) will give you freedom - knowing that they are noted and will be dealt with.

Travel

As a business owner or entrepreneur, chances are pretty good that you are going to do a lot of traveling. Planning and booking a business trip is far from being an easy or exciting task. Fortunately, travel booking is one of the many tasks that you can delegate to your VA.

But first, ask yourself 'Do I really need to travel?' Ok, if you are delivering a workshop that needs to be done face-to-face that's a no brainer, but you may habitually hop on a train to London for a monthly meeting when actually you could consider doing it via Skype. Just because meetings have been held at the same hotel on the 2nd Tuesday of the month for the last 10 years doesn't necessarily mean they need to continue this way. In fact, quite the opposite. Is it not time that you were challenging this and suggesting an alternative way, saving money and time in the process? You may get resistance from some people initially, but stick to your guns, ask them to bear with you and just try it once or twice. You'll often find that once they realise that it's not that bad and they've saved themselves hours of time travelling, not to mention the cost of the travel, they'll be on board.

But if you do have to travel, it's important to use your travel time effectively – make calls on hands-free whilst you're driving, dictate emails, reports, blogs, quotes (hands free of course) into a phone App or dictaphone. If you have just come from a meeting or appointment, dictate the actions required. These may be a quote for work, a proposal, a confirmation letter, a follow up email, etc. You can save for later for adding to your To-Do list when you are not driving, or simply email the audio file to your VA to transcribe.

Consider using travel time as an opportunity to learn. *Earners are learners... leaders are readers* and all that. Listen to audio books and podcasts. At the time of writing this, Audible.co.uk has a great offer where you pay a small monthly fee - discounted for the first few months - and for that you can download an audio book every month. They also offer various discounts and 'coupons' on an on-going basis. Go onto their online chat and ask for one!

If you travel away on business regularly, it's useful to keep a pre-packed overnight bag. Double-up on toiletries, notepads, pens, mobile phone charger, underwear, and any other essentials that you can pack in advance. Keep a short checklist of items to add. If you want to be uber organised, you can keep a laminated copy of that checklist in the bag itself. On the checklist you may want to include the likes of: sat nav (if driving), laptop with charger, sunglasses (for driving), mobile phone, notes for trip/meeting, etc.

The night before you go, half of your bag is already packed and the other half is simply a case of ticking off a checklist and throwing them in. You'll be done and dusted in a couple of minutes!

"Concentrate all your thoughts upon the work at hand. The sun's rays do not burn until brought to a focus"
Alexander Graham Bell

CHAPTER 4
To-Do List

Now, I don't necessarily want to promote the word "obsessed" but to be honest, the secret of getting things done *is* to become a little bit obsessed by your To-Do list. Live it, breathe it, work through it relentlessly. Visualise today's tasks completed. Don't be afraid to refer to it continuously throughout the day, to maintain your focus. The desire to get to the end of it will focus your mind like never before.

But let's keep a healthy balance here. Focus on your tasks during your work hours; don't obsess about your To-Do list when you're supposed to be chilling with the family!

Do I Need a To-Do List?

Tell me to get a life, but I've spent a lot of time over the years looking at different ways people keep track of what they need to do.

I've been intrigued by the differing views on whether you should have a To-Do list, in what format, with how many items on it, a list format vs. mindmap-style. And I've listened to the argument of why you *shouldn't* have one (it doesn't help with long term memory, etc.) I've observed a disorganised colleague struggle by without one ("I will *never* have a To-do list, I *refuse!*") - missing birthdays, losing paperwork, double-booking engagements and overlooking appointments. It's a pretty stressful existence.

My conclusion is that you should have a To-Do list. To truly relax, you need to be confident that every task is on your radar - captured somewhere and won't be overlooked.

And your To-Do list should really be online. Why? Well for a start you can't lose it. You can update it on the fly and when you get back to your desk, it's already synched to your computer. Cracking. I'll cover what online software I recommend in Chapter 7.

Efficiently Managing your To-Do list

Your To-Do list will become the central point of your working day – the one place where everything is captured and prioritised.

You should by now be in the habit of questioning every task you do and whether it forms part of your overall goals. One of the best times to do this is just as you are about to add it onto your To-Do list. If you absolutely have to do it and it *is* part of your goals, is there someone else that you can delegate it to? If it's not appropriate to delegate it, question to what standard does it have to be done? Will you get away with a less than perfect job? The answer to that should almost always be yes.

Never have more than ten To-Do items on your To-Do list for one day. Any more than this is likely to be unrealistic and can cause overwhelm, negatively impacting your productivity and potentially causing you to procrastinate.

Of those ten, a maximum of three should be tasks that if you do absolutely nothing else you must get these done today. This will force your focus on these three tasks. Make sure you tackle them in the morning.

First thing each morning, scan down your To-Do list. Re-familiarise yourself with it briefly - then if you are sat for example, in a traffic jam, on your way to a meeting or on hold on the phone, you can start to give it some thought. You'll find it much easier to dive into a task if you already know *how* you are going to tackle it – this is half the battle of overcoming procrastination.

Assign each task a High, Medium or Low priority:

- **High** is for tasks where there will be consequences for not doing them. These may be tasks such as calling a potential client back or meeting with an existing client.
- **Medium** would be something that you should do, but if you don't, the consequences won't be as severe as if you didn't do a High priority task.
- **Low** doesn't particularly have any immediate consequences if you don't do it. It may be a pleasant task that will need doing eventually, but there is no immediate urgency for.

Always be mindful that you shouldn't tick something off your To-Do list without considering the next actions required. Does it require a follow up? Remember that as soon as you remove it from your list, unless it's a recurring task, it will fall into a black hole.

Keep focused by regularly checking your To-Do list throughout the day. This constant reminder is a great way of keeping you focused and on track with what you need to accomplish.

There are some things that if you don't do them there and then, at that moment, you know deep inside that they just won't get done. Has that happened to you? Recognise that gut feeling and if that task only takes a few minutes, do it now! If it will take longer than a few minutes, take a few seconds out of your day (that's all it takes) to add it to your To-Do list.

Keep it on your Radar

Be careful that you don't let things fall off your radar.

As I mentioned above, the classic case of this is you complete an item on your To-Do list, which is only half of the overall task, but you don't add another item to follow up the outcome. For example, you may be completing a job for a client. Your To-Do list may say 'Create Facebook page for Client A'. So you create the Facebook page, email the details to the client asking them to check they are happy with it and tick it off your To-Do list.

The client would like a couple of changes but they are so busy that they don't get back to you. You have no mechanism in place to follow-up as it's fallen off your radar. You look inefficient to your client for not following up, and if you have a super-slick invoicing system in place, the client may get invoiced for the work before it has been completed.

Either way, it's not looking good for your business: not only do you acquire a disgruntled client, but your business appears disorganised and unprofessional.

Another common cause of tasks falling off your radar is when you delegate them. This is a good time to use your To-Do list for following up. Although it can be frustrating that you have to chase people, in reality even the most efficient of us overlook tasks. Adding a quick follow up task is a safety net that I recommend you use with people who have a track record of missing deadlines or people whom you don't know well enough yet to know if they're dependable.

Future To-Dos

Adding To-Do items for the future is a fabulous little trick, which I use all the time. My life has been so much easier since I started doing this. I'll give you an example.

Let's say you ask someone to stand in for you next week at a meeting or pick your kids up from school. They are happy to oblige but have asked for a reminder nearer the time. Or perhaps they have let you down in the past and you feel that you'd like to give them a reminder.

Type straight onto your To-Do list:

'Hi Alison, I hope it's still ok to [collect Sophie from school / stand in for me at the 2pm meeting] later. Any probs let me know'. Then assign it to the day it is happening and assign it a top priority. And forget about it. On the day, it pops up as one of the first items on your To-Do list – you copy & paste it straight onto a text first thing in the morning and hit send. Job done.

Likewise, if you borrow an item from somebody and they tell you they need it back by the end of the month, again add a 'To-Do' item: *'Return book to Rachel'* and assign it a date later in the month. Then forget about it.

Recurring To-Dos

Recurring To-Do items are a great way of not letting on-going tasks fall off your radar.

You can have them pop up weekly, monthly, annually, the last Tuesday of the month, the second Friday of the month, whatever you choose.

Examples of what they might be are:

- Check client emails (daily)
- Review team task list (weekly)
- Produce agenda for Skype progress call (monthly).

These are examples of when recurring To-Dos come into their own. Whatever the task, no matter how small, add it on to make sure it gets done.

You can also use recurring reminders for Birthdays, Anniversaries or any other regular dates you need to remember. To be super-efficient, for a birthday you may choose to add two recurring reminders to your To-Do list – one 7 days before the event reminding you to buy a card or gift, and one for the actual day to wish that person a happy birthday – for example: *'Happy Birthday Kate! Have a wonderful day'.* Each year it pops up on Kate's birthday and you simply copy and paste into a text and hit send. A great way to earn brownie points!

Be Explicit

When adding a task to your To-Do list, it's important to be explicit about what needs to be done.

For example, rather than adding a single word as a reminder (e.g. "Blog"), try "Write draft blog post on top 5 time saving apps". It's quite possible that "Blog" has been sat on your To-Do list for a while as it requires some thought to decipher the first action.

If you give a few seconds thought to the first action required when adding a task to your list, it will add clarity and help get it done more quickly.

In Chapter 10 we cover in more detail how to chunk tasks down effectively.

Close Off your To-Do list

Once you get into the swing of it, you'll prepare your To-Do list the night before.

This list should remain static. On the day, don't add anything else unless it is truly urgent. By allowing tasks to be added on throughout the day you water-down the focus that you created the night before when you were preparing that list. Your day's work starts to become more overwhelming and less achievable.

Instead, when asked to do something, manage people's expectations by telling them it won't be done today, but it will be prioritised accordingly.

Quickly add it onto your To-Do list for tomorrow. When your working day has finished and you are planning for tomorrow (see 'Plan for Tomorrow' section), you can decide then whether it will actually be completed tomorrow or not. But you can forget about it for now – it's been captured.

How did you do Today?

At the end of every working day, revisit your To-Do list.

On a *really* good day this will be completely clear as you've accomplished all tasks on it.

On a good day, your To-Do list may have a couple of tasks left on there. Firstly, congratulate yourself on achieving what you have done. Then look at what was not achieved today and why. Can you do anything differently tomorrow? Maybe, maybe not.

On a not-so-good day there may be 5 or more tasks (of your maximum of 10) left on there. Don't beat yourself up about it. Instead, be proactive - look at what factors stopped you from achieving more and how can you stop that from happening again. Did you give yourself an unrealistic workload? What interruptions did you have? Could you have prevented them? Were you firm enough in saying 'no'? Or perhaps you just weren't feeling motivated today.

There's a whole chapter further on about working through unproductive periods. There's also a chapter about dealing with interruptions. By the time you've come to the end of this book, if you choose to apply the techniques and guidance offered, you'll most definitely be a highly organised, focused and more profitable business owner.

Make it your absolute mission to clear that To-Do list tomorrow.

Plan for Tomorrow

At the end of each day it's always a good idea to review your To-Do list for tomorrow.

What's left from today, if anything, will need to be transferred onto another day. But don't leave it overdue. If it has now become urgent then assign it the highest priority for tomorrow. Otherwise assign it to another day. As long as it's not showing as overdue. Method in my madness? Yes. If you are constantly working through a list with overdue items on, aside from feeling like you're starting every day on the back foot, it's no good for your motivation levels. Start each day with a fresh slate.

Next, look at your calendar – how much time do you have available to do these tasks?

Make sure that it's achievable in line with your availability. Is it realistic considering the meetings and appointments you have on? For example, if you have to travel to a 3 hour meeting, then back for a dental appointment, it's completely unreasonable to think that you're going to be able to write a lengthy report, pull together a PowerPoint presentation, call six clients, design a spreadsheet and review your terms and conditions. Unless you have extraordinary powers.

This is where prioritisation really comes into its own. You need to be incredibly ruthless here. What are the high value tasks on your list? In other words, which tasks will create the most value by being done? And most importantly double-check that every single task on there is in line with your overall goals and roles. If not, kick it out! Questioning if a task is in line with your goals will become habitual after a while. If it's not, it won't even make it onto your To-Do list in the first place. And don't forget the delegation factor - before it even gets to your To-Do list, you should have determined whether the item can be delegated to another team member or to your VA.

Once you've decided on an achievable list, clear the decks and hide everything that does not relate to the tasks on that list. The old 'out of sight, out of mind' applies. It will increase your focus. Get any paperwork or notes that relate to the tasks and put them in the 'To-Do Today' section of your organisation file so they are to hand when you need them tomorrow.

By creating and reviewing your list the night before, your brain will process it during sleep. It won't affect your sleep, but you'll wake with a feeling of acquaintance with the tasks and sometimes with some great ideas and insights. You'll feel more in control of your day.

Tip: The night before, prepare the things you will need for the day and leave by the front door. There's nothing worse than a last minute dash to find your files that you need for the meeting you should have left for 5 minutes ago.

In Chapter 1 in the 'Clear Your Mind' section, I asked you to write down all those stray thoughts running around in your head, so that we could clear them. If you recall these weren't necessarily tasks – they could be decisions you need to make (what to do with a contractor who isn't performing, which school to send your children to, best invoicing system to use, and so on).

I'd like you to put that list in front of you now, and add all items on it to your online To-Do list. There you go – all captured.

*"Focus on being productive
instead of busy"
Timothy Ferriss,
The 4-Hour Workweek*

CHAPTER 5
Emails

Love them or hate them, you can't deny that emails are an excellent communication tool.

However, they are equally the bane of our lives. Invading our inboxes in such volume, distracting our focus. Good news, bad news, surprises, bombshells. New clients, old friends, Viagra, SEO experts from India chancing their luck. The must-have gadgets, the latest apps, second-guessing Google's latest algorithms, the not-to-be-missed webinar to grow your business by 129%.

So, how do you effectively manage this diverse barrage of information without it taking over your day? I figured this warranted a chapter all of its own.

Step 1 – Transfer to Gmail

I can't recommend Gmail highly enough. Having used many different email clients over the years, I was astounded by the amount of time I saved through using Gmail. If you don't already use it, you should set up an account today - it's free and easy. If you already have a Gmail account, make sure you have all of your emails coming into it – both business and personal. You can set it up to send and receive emails from any email address.

What's so good about Gmail?

Gmail has the best spam filter ever. Its intelligence still wows me now – it seems to know better than I do if something is spam or not. I've never gone into my spam folder and found anything that shouldn't be there.

As it's a creation of Google, Gmail has a superb search facility that allows you to find emails instantly without having to trawl. Nothing less than you would expect from a Google search.

The amount of storage you have means that you can store a large volume of emails. Gmail has a fabulous 'Archive' option – this takes emails out of your inbox but keeps them so that when you search, you can access them instantly.

Have you ever sent an email and as soon as you hit 'send' wished you hadn't? Gmail allows you to 'undo' an email being sent for a short period after you've hit the send button. It's got me out of many a scrape. Just make sure that you enable this in settings.

Gmail is constantly introducing experimental add-ons that you can opt to try. It comes under the 'Labs' feature – there are some real gems in there. It's worth keeping your eye on this to check out the latest improvements.

An addition to Gmail, which caused controversy with email marketers when it was first introduced, is the segregation of emails into pre-determined categories (tabs of your inbox), the main ones being: Primary, Social and Promotions. I share the concern of email marketers (we do email marketing too) and can understand why open rates declined somewhat as a result of Google doing this. However, putting that aside for a minute, and looking at this purely from the perspective of what I am helping you with - streamlining your work and increasing your daily focus - this categorisation from Google is an absolute godsend. It puts the social media updates (Social) and the newsletters (Promotions) under their own tabs and out of direct view, allowing you to focus on the important emails (Primary).

Gmail integrates with Google+. Even if you are not a fan of Google+, if you have a business, (at the time of writing this) it's good to be actively on there.

There are plenty more benefits which you will find out for yourself.

Step 2 – Cut down on email volume

Unsubscribe

There is a ton of useful material out there that lands in your inbox in the form of newsletters. You could easily spend all day, every day reading it if you choose to. But that's just not practical. So, have a reality check and let's go for quality over quantity. Choose the top few real informative newsletters – that could be practical tips that you can implement in your business, information that develops you or industry updates for your field. In short, material that adds value.

The classic inbox bomber is Groupon. People who can't resist a bargain fight through this mass of daily -or twice daily – emails then buy something for the sake of it (see *Consequences of Choice* in Chapter 3 on actions attracting effort). Don't fall into this time-consuming trap.

Your first job is to unsubscribe from everything you possibly

can. Make that your immediate mission this week. Simply find and hit the unsubscribe option on the email and you're done. It's normally at the bottom of the email in small text, but sometimes it's at the top.

Don't just "delete" the email because tomorrow, next week or next month - another one will be back in your inbox. It's worth taking the time to "unsubscribe" - and then "delete".

If this makes you nervous, as a comfort blanket, create a Label for those emails that you don't want to unsubscribe from and call it 'Read later'. Then create a Filter to take it out of your inbox before it even arrives. These emails are there if you get time to read them but somehow I doubt you will.

Don't get involved in chain emails

The biggest waste of time and energy are chain and 'joke' emails.

The most exasperating of all come from superstitious beings who genuinely believe that, as the email says, if you don't forward it to at least 20 people within 24 hours you will have bad luck. So guess what? They pass that onto you to deal with as one of their 20. Thanks for that. And... deeee-lete.

Ask your family and friends firmly not to send you these types of emails. I did this about 3 or 4 years ago. I'm sure I did offend a couple of more sensitive souls at the time, but they got over it without any dramas and I've not had any since. Job done!

Minimise questions from potential customers

If you don't have one already, look at adding a Frequently Asked Questions (FAQs) section to your website. It's important that your website is intuitive. If you use a good online marketer they will tell you that you need to visit every page of your website in the shoes of your customer – what might they be looking for next, what's going to trigger them to call or email, what page will they click on next, what are they looking for, at what point are they ready to buy, are they looking for more information to build up trust. And so on.

In case you're wondering, this section hasn't inadvertently ended up in this book. I'm not coming at this from an online marketing perspective, but a view of time saving and work streamlining. Aside from this being a key part of your marketing strategy, if your website answers questions potential customers may have, this will reduce the number of enquiries you receive into your inbox.

Step 3 – Therapy

Create a Label (or folder) and call it 'Old Emails'.

OK, are you ready for this?

Move the *whole* contents of your inbox into there (for Gmail apply the Label then Archive). Bob's your Uncle – a completely clear inbox. How good does that feel?

Stop twitching.

Out of sight, out of mind. It will massively reduce your level of distractions and will provide a clean slate to start afresh with a manageable inbox. Once you move the entire contents out of your inbox and apply my recommendations for dealing with all new incoming emails, checking emails is suddenly much less of a deal and your inbox is back to zero daily.

Now, add a recurring task onto your To-Do list to clear 5 emails a day from your 'Old Emails' folder (see *5-a-day* in Chapter 10).

Step 4 - Organise your Inbox

As I mentioned above, Gmail have already made a great start by taking any spam out of the equation and by categorising your inbox so the most relevant information is put immediately in front of you. You've helped to narrow that down further by ruthlessly unsubscribing from everything that didn't make it into the top few newsletters that add the most value to you and your business. So that's a great start, but there is more you can do yet.

Grouping Conversations (Called Threads in iOS)

To make sure you visually have the least number of emails, and for convenient access, make sure your email settings are set to group conversations (Gmail will automatically apply this setting). In other words, if an email is sent back and forth all the replies will group together in one place and look like one email. You can easily click into this to access the separate replies.

Using Filters

A few minutes spent building a smart system using Gmail's Filters and Labels will make the messages coming into your inbox as relevant as possible, letting you focus on what's really important.

Gmail's Filters are similar to Outlook's Rules - based on pre-defined criteria, you can automatically label, archive, delete, star, or forward your mail before it even appears in your inbox. Gmail's Labels help to organise mail into your own categories - similar to Folders in Outlook, except you can apply more than one to any given message. For example, you may want to keep a record of Amazon emails, but you certainly don't need your inbox clogged up with an entourage of emails when you're trying to focus ('your order has been received'... 'your order is being processed'... 'your order has been dispatched'.)

One very effective way I use Filters is that I ask my team to copy me in on all outgoing emails and I receive a copy of all incoming ones too. They automatically divert to a 'Client Correspondence' subfolder of my inbox, which takes me only a few minutes to scan through at the end of each day. I remember to do this by having a recurring daily task (Mon-Fri) on my To-Do list (with a low priority, so I don't see it until the end of the day).

These emails then don't distract me during the day but do allow me to stay aware of what's going on, identify any issues promptly (and sometimes before they happen) and allows me to see where any given job is up to if the client contacts me directly or if the team member dealing with it is off.

What emails can you divert out of your inbox?

Segregating business and personal emails

I recommend that you have all of your emails - regardless of the email address - coming into the same email client (Gmail preferably), as it saves you time not having to log into more than one place to access different emails.

For personal emails, have them divert into a subfolder of your inbox for dealing with separately – outside of your work hours. Ask your friends and family to always use your personal email address. If they realise that their email will be looked at quicker if it is sent to your business address, they may try this. If they do, simply drag it into the subfolder where your personal emails go to deal with later. When you do deal with it later, make sure you reply using your personal email address. It's subtle training for your family and friends!

When signing up to receive newsletters for non-business use, purchasing online goods, registering non work-related software or guarantees, and other such times where you have to register an email address, remember to always use your personal one.

Using Out of Office to your advantage

Consider using an 'out of office' auto response to manage customer expectations.

This can be used to acknowledge receipt and specify a timeframe when you will get back to the client. It takes the pressure off having to check your emails permanently throughout the day and they know where they stand.

May I suggest something along the lines of:

"Thank you for your email. This inbox is checked Monday to Friday twice daily – at around 10am and 3pm. If your email requires a more urgent response please call XXXX and we will be happy to help."

Step 5 - Checking Emails

Have an on-going goal to maintain an empty inbox (or 'inbox zero') by the end of each day.

When to check emails

It may be easier to start with when *not* to check emails.

Never check emails first thing when you are at your most creative. It will impact your productivity for the day a lot more than you would think. And you'll risk losing your strategy and implementation time (*Daily Implementation Time*, Chapter 1).

Assign a set block of time to deal with emails and stick to it. Do this twice a day and where possible at the same times every day. Save any emails that you need to send for this dedicated time. Close your email down at all other times.

A great time to check emails is around 10am – this way you pick up anything urgent pretty quickly in the morning, but it doesn't distract you from your priorities for the day.

Another good time is late afternoon. You catch anything that has come in since 10am when you last checked and it still gives you enough time to acknowledge anything pressing.

One at a time

Remember the one-touch rule. Don't scan down your emails cherry-picking – start at the top. Read the newest first, as you may find that some have already been dealt with, or that there have been replies from other people included in the email.

Work down, one at a time doing one of the following:

- Delete
- Unsubscribe then delete
- Archive (if you don't need to action but may need to access at a later date)
- If it needs actioning, put it on your To-Do list then Archive. It's no longer clogging your inbox or your headspace but it's on your radar and therefore will get done. You can forget about it for now (remember you can copy the Gmail web link & paste it straight onto your To-Do list)
- Reply quickly (then use Gmail's wonderful 'send and archive' button)

   NB: before you hit 'send and archive', do a quick mental check – is any follow up required? It if is, copy & paste the Gmail web link for that particular email into your To-Do list before you hit the button and send it into a black hole

- If it's a small task (only a minute or two), action there and then, then archive once done.

Don't reply to everything

Only reply to emails that you need to. Often you will simply be copied in for information only. No response is needed. And often someone will simply be sending you an update. Again no need to reply.

Make sure you set the expectations of those who work with you that you won't be responding to information only emails, so if they require a response they will need to specifically ask for one.

Effective Responses

When replying to emails, keep it short and to the point. This is empowering for a number of reasons.

If you write essays on email, you'll associate email checking with a long arduous process and therefore experience a feeling of dread every time you need to check your emails. You need to get this twice-daily chore condensed down to a manageable quick and easy process that you can effortlessly work through that results in your inbox being zero.

And if an email chain is bouncing back & forth and getting nowhere, pick up the phone! Before you do though, jot the main points down. Keep to the point and don't waste their time. Or yours.

Working late again

No matter how many times I harp on about work life balance, you're not going to completely listen to me. I know that. You're an entrepreneur right? This makes you a likely candidate to be a workaholic.

So I won't pretend that we entrepreneurs never work late. But just one word of advice. Never let people *know* you work late. As soon as they find out this, the boundaries change. Your after hours peace to complete a task without interruption suddenly becomes fair game. People start to wonder why you've not replied to an email that they sent you in the evening and you find your phone ringing well into the evening.

If you are sending emails late at night, either put them in drafts so that you (or your VA) can simply hit send in the morning. Or you could use a handy – albeit a little pricey – tool called Boomerang. It works in conjunction with Gmail and allows you to send emails at specified times. If you are working late, you could set the email to go out at 7am the following day, for example.

Boomerang also means you can send a recurring email, which I found excellent for reminding my team to send their monthly timesheets and monthly expense sheets. You set it up once and the same email goes out every month without any intervention required. How's that for efficiency?

Increase your chances of receiving a prompt response

To make sure people act quickly when responding to your emails, make sure you are concise and to the point. Keep pleasantries to a minimum; you don't want your request to get lost in the wording.

Say what you need, how and by when in the opening sentence. Bang! Your message just got through loud and clear. Then provide any additional information that is necessary underneath that.

Use "FYI only" if you don't need the person to respond.

If you are sending the email to more than one person, you need to be even more specific about what you need each person to do. For example:

Hi Emma, Please can you finish the HSBC presentation by 2pm tomorrow and 'reply all' to this email so that Stacey and John receive a copy too.

Stacey/John - Please can I have your feedback on the presentation by email by 5pm tomorrow.

Gareth – FYI only.

Thanks.

Choose your subject line carefully. If it's urgent, imagine you're writing a headline for your next e-newsletter. Make it snappy, and attention-grabbing so that it stands out from the sea of emails. Don't be shy in putting the deadline in the headline!

HSBC Presentation: Deadline 2pm 11th Feb

If you don't receive a reply, re-forward the same email with a short polite covering email, such as:

Hi Emma, I know you're busy, but I just want to make sure you received my email below and are on track for the presentation deadline of 2pm. Please drop me a quick email by 1pm to confirm?

Thanks.

Day not going according to plan?

Of course sometimes your day will go Pete Tong and you may get a little behind on clearing your inbox.

If this happens, always focus on keeping on top of today's emails. Scan down them to check there is nothing important or from a client. If there is, these should be prioritised – add them to your To-Do list and if necessary send a brief acknowledgement.

For everything left, move them to your 'Old Emails' folder. Remember that? The one we mass transferred the contents of your inbox into. The chances are they're not important and if they are, someone will come back to you.

OK, you're right back to inbox zero!

Ditch that guilt. You are only human – you can't reply to every single email that you receive. That person will chase you if it's important. Otherwise you'll pick it up eventually in your 5-a-day (see *5-a-day*, Chapter 10).

Have your emails checked for you

Consider having a Virtual Assistant check your emails. This can be highly efficient and free up your time to spend on more important tasks such as growing your business.

Or it can be a time-sapper.

It simply depends on two things – the proficiency of your VA and your relationship with them. Choose carefully - if they are skilled, show initiative and you invest some time in building a relationship, after a while they will be responding to your emails just as you would – but in less time than it takes you.

Once or twice each day, a VA can sort your emails into folders such as 'Urgent' and 'Queries'. They can delete and archive the stuff you don't need to see and add tasks onto your To-Do list to retain a zero inbox. They can even draft replies for you to check & hit send. And when you get comfortable with them, they can reply without you needing to check it first. You'll be surprised at how quickly a good VA will pick up on what's urgent / important and how to reply, etc.

If it takes, say, 15 minutes each day for a VA to check your emails (that's 1.25 hours @ an average rate of £22/hour = £27.50/week). Worth every penny if you don't need to stress about them.

Tim Ferriss, author of The 4-hour Work Week uses his no-nonsense approach to sum it up - albeit lacking charm:

"No one can check my e-mail for me".   Get over yourself. Checking e-mail isn't some amazing skill that you alone possess.

"My own business always bores me to death; I prefer other people's"
Oscar Wilde

CHAPTER 6
Networking

Network with a clear goal in mind. But have patience.

Networking. Yuk. One of my personal pet hates.

Don't get me wrong, I'm not another Morrissey. I do actually *love* people. They fascinate me and I'm genuinely interested in learning about them and their businesses. But given the choice I'd prefer doing this in my own time and at my own pace. So being thrown together with essentially strangers for a short burst of time doesn't really set the scene for a relaxed natural conversation for me.

I rarely meet anyone who genuinely enjoys traditional networking. But I accept it's necessary in business. So I'm going to share with you my views on how to get the most out of it.

And so that you don't only have my cynical view on this, I've also asked my colleague, Susan Miller, who hosts the Free2Network Chester events for her take on how to get the most out of networking.

In line with the theme of this book, the angle I'm coming from with my tips and advice on networking is purely time saving, focus and maximising efficiency. Here goes...

Select the meetings you attend carefully. Don't remain in your comfort zone by going to the ones you feel comfortable at. Push yourself out of that comfort zone – keep focused on the ultimate purpose of networking – to get business.

Find out if there is an attendee list available to you. Some events will issue this prior to the event. If there is, have a look through – who is attending that you want to speak with? Introduce yourself beforehand to them via email or LinkedIn explaining a little about what you do, and saying you'd like to hear more about what they do.

Create standard wording for messages of this nature, so you can simply copy & paste it into a message adding the person's name. If you use Gmail (which I highly recommend, see Chapter 5) you can use the fabulous 'canned response' function for this.

When you are there, cut to the chase. Have a clear goal in your mind of what you want to get out of it. By the way, I'm not advocating talking *at* people about what you do in a hard-faced sales pitch kind of a way. I don't believe you get anything from that. On the contrary, by simply listening to people I have picked up a lot more work. I've also been able to identify early warning signals of people I quite frankly don't want to work with. It takes time to build relationships, so persisting with the same network groups - once you have identified which are likely to be most effective – is a wise decision. But do be a network tart. As long as you have persisted for a reasonable number of meetings, if one group doesn't prove to be fruitful, try another one.

So when I talk about having a clear goal in mind, that could be as simple as "speak to John Taylor and Jenny Ashton". If you do nothing else at that session, you will be focused on speaking to them. Your goal should certainly not be getting through as many people as humanly possible in the room and collecting enough business cards to start a bonfire.

Make your goal simple, clear and achievable. Remember that relationships take time to build. Don't plough in there and frighten people off. According to research, people need to spend on average 7 hours with you before they'll build enough trust to buy from you or recommend you.

If an attendee list isn't available, introduce yourself to the organiser on arrival. Explain what you do and ask for introductions to any relevant business owners.

Make sure your 40 or 60 second pitch is perfected. It should sound natural, be captivating and talk to the pain of your potential clients. For example, if you are an IT consultant, you may refer to a statistic of the amount of hours small business owners waste by not backing up their files often enough.

When someone asks what you do, you can simply reel it off without thinking too hard about it. Bish bash bosh.

And it should actually be 40 or 60 seconds. Each network will have a prescribed length for your introduction. Don't go over – this can give the impression to others that you are disorganised or inefficient. Not only that but it prolongs the 'round robin' process, which in turn delays you getting out of there on time!

I sometimes set a precedent when I arrive at networking meetings by saying that I may have to leave a little early. It gives me the option to do exactly that if it's not going well or it's not beneficial. Fake that incoming text asking you to be somewhere, make your excuses and leave. A little white lie in this instance is harmless and kinder than the truth *("your networking meetings are rubbish")*.

And now, to balance out my scepticism, here is Sue's advice...

I understand Sarah's reluctance to attend networking sessions on a regular basis. Done haphazardly, networking can be a big waste of time. However, my experience as both a regular attendee and a host is that it can work! If you're new at networking, take the next month and plan to attend one a week, or at the bare minimum, two that month. There is a plethora of regular networking events in most areas so first you need to find one that suits you. (I suggest for now, you join only 1 group). Some are more relaxed than others. The costs to attend vary - as well as the times. What suits you best? Are you able to attend meetings at 7 o'clock in the morning or do you prefer a time during school hours? Keep in mind that if it is a breakfast or lunch meeting, you will be paying for your food on top of your networking fee. Personally, I prefer the mid-morning events where the only extra cost is my choice of beverage. I want to make connections, not share a meal with people I don't know very well.

There is one very simple key to getting a return on investment from networking: attend regularly. As Sarah said above, on average, you need to spend time with someone for 7 hours before they trust you enough to do business with you. By becoming a member of your preferred networking group, and attending on a regular basis, you will soon get to know not just one person, but several. Those of you who are committed to your networking group will naturally support each other. I have seen it time and time again. If you pop in to a group and don't get any business on your first or second visit so never come again - you are out of sight and out of mind. Networking will not work for you with this approach.

I try to attend a minimum of 3 (preferably 4) per month. I simply put the dates in my diary for the next 3 months and I attend. With travel time, this takes approximately 2 hours per session. The group I belong to allows members to attend any of their events in the North West at no extra charge. This means I am seeing many regulars (building my relationships) as well as meeting some newcomers at different venues. If I'm travelling a distance, then I always book a 1-to-1 after the formal networking with someone I know is attending. Booking 1-to-1 meetings with people you meet at events is the second most important rule of successful networking!

I also find networking with your member group a great confidence booster. You can perfect your "pitch" among friends, your conversation comfort zone improves, you have interaction with other entrepreneurs (particularly important if you work from home without much regular people contact) and you garner new ideas that could very well invigorate you and your business.

If you approach networking with the view to help others, you will find you will be rewarded - just have patience. Do not push your business on others - you will be trusted more if you are offering to help others with leads, offering advice, sharing knowledge. The old adage "what goes around, comes around" is never more true than in networking.

This book is all about being efficient. My advice is to treat networking as a serious rung on your marketing ladder and you will achieve results. Plan, execute and follow-up.

Here are my top tips for successful networking:

1. Attend the same group regularly (minimum twice a month)

2. Book 1-to-1 meetings with people you meet through networking

3. Always attend networking events with your business cards and your diary

4. Give, give, give and you *shall* receive

5. Build a relationship first. Ask questions, listen for the opportunity.

6. Be reliable - and be prepared.

*Susan is a Cheshire host for www.free2network.co.uk

Managing Business Cards

Business cards have a wonderful purpose. But only if used properly. Implement a process to deal with any new business cards you are given and you can prevent them popping up all over the place – in the bottom of your handbag... stuffed in your wallet... in pockets of various clothing (discovered a few weeks later).

OK, as you can probably predict, I'm going to suggest you are pretty ruthless with the business cards you receive. There'll be ones that you asked for, ones that were forced upon you and ones that you've accepted purely out of politeness.

Deal with these cards as soon as you return to the office, don't leave them lying around – remember the one touch rule.

Firstly, bin any that you have no use for. Merciless as that sounds, it has to be done. Set aside your thoughts on how much money it must have cost to produce such a snazzy business card (if it is) or how pleasant the person was to talk to. If that person or their business doesn't fit into your vision and goals, it's curtains for that business card. It's probably fair to say that most of the 'forced upon you' and 'accepted out of politeness' business cards will fit into this category.

And for goodness sake don't feel guilty about binning multiple business cards from the same person if they fall into this same category. If you had wanted to be a delivery boy/girl when you grew up you would have set up in that business - it's not good practice for people to give you a large handful of their business cards asking you to forward them onto as many people as you can think of. So, unless it's reciprocal, or their business aligns with your vision and goals, bin them without guilt.

That leaves the ones that you are genuinely interested in. But just to be sure - revisit the ultimate question: *Are the opportunities with this person/business in line with my goals and vision?* If that person is a potential client, this is clearly a yes. If you can refer business to each other or there is scope for a joint venture, that's another yes. And there may be business cards in there that you think a particular family member, friend or business colleague would be interested in. Try not to invent your own 'just in case' category.

Other than that, you may find that you lose a few more at this stage. This just leaves you with the business cards of genuine interest. For each one, determine what you *ultimately* want to achieve – it may be to acquire a new client, to launch a JV (Joint Venture) or there could be other desired outcomes.

Send a follow up email (or ask your VA to). You can use a canned response (if you use Gmail) or the equivalent. You may choose to personalise it (I would recommend this) by simply adding the person's name and one extra sentence in.

The sentence could be, for example: *'Thanks for recommending [book name], I'm looking forward to reading it'* or *'I wish your daughter luck with her exam'* or *'Thanks for the recommendation of a web designer, etc. etc.* In the canned response, I'd suggest you ask if they would be happy to be added to your mailing list. If they are, the auto-responder sequence will kick in, automating the contact with these people but still keeping you in the forefront of their mind.

If you have a CRM system, add the businesses you'd like to acquire as clients onto here. If not, either add them onto a prospects spreadsheet - which you regularly review - to track the progress, or onto your To-Do list as a follow up note.

You may want to capture notes relating to each one – such as where you met the person or the context in which you met them, how they can help your business, how you can help their business, what they do and any special or unique things about that person – or their business - which can be used to maintain the relationship in the future. You can also store other random information, for example, how to pronounce their name.

You may want to use a business card scanner App to capture those contact details. Searching for "business card scanner app" or similar will turn up several options. Evernote is a good option.

Once the details from the business cards have been captured, you can throw them away. If you prefer to keep them (which I don't recommend), you could file them either in a business card holder book, A4 plastic wallets for business cards (stored in your meeting folder) or rolodex-style storage.

"Organize around business functions, not people. Build systems within each business function. Let systems run the business and people run the systems. People come and go but the systems remain constant"
Michael Gerber, The E-Myth Revisited

CHAPTER 7
Systems

The secret to an efficiently run business is structure and consistency. To achieve this, it's simple – you build your business as if you're planning to franchise it. In *The E-Myth Revisited*, Michael Gerber looks at the success of McDonalds - 'the most successful small business in the world' - and why their franchise model is so successful.

It brings home that overused, but spot-on, phrase about working *on* your business, not *in* your business. Michael talks about detaching yourself from your business and allowing it to run efficiently without you, through systematisation and providing structure to the people who work for you. It's a superb read that provokes thought, and ideas that will make you look at your business in a way you never have before. I would highly recommend it.

You need systems in place to make your business function without you in it. By systems I mean software systems, hardware, manual processes. Everything that happens in your business should have a set process and be documented in a manual.

It's impossible to cover all scenarios of manual processes (or desktop procedures as they are sometimes known), so in this chapter I'm going to concentrate on software (and some hardware) that I've tried and tested, that will help systemise your business and help to make it run more efficiently.

Review your Existing Systems

It's a useful exercise to take time to review all the systems you have in place – or not in place as the case may be. Find new systems to make your routines slicker. This process can take a long time, it can be an arduous process, but it's absolutely worth it.

A tip to cut through the mountain of information available online when looking for software - go to a LinkedIn group of like-minded people whom you trust and put your question out there: *"Can anyone recommend a system for invoicing clients? It must do X, Y and preferably Z."* As well as outlining your high-level requirements, you may also want to provide additional information such as your budget.

You'll often find that people have been through the same process themselves and are very happy to share their experiences. As well as being useful, it saves you a stack of time researching.

Amongst the processes to implement, you'll need a well-organised system that captures any orders or new client requests and tracks them right through the process to conversion. It will include regular reviews to make sure you're on track. Once they become a client, you will need to make sure you invoice them promptly, reply to their emails within 24 hours if possible (except for weekends of course). Your business needs to come across as organised, efficient and professional. This will give your customers confidence that you'll deliver and they'll come back for more. Always give realistic expectations to customers, but make sure you *do* give expectations. There's a lot to cover, and it all needs to be captured in your systems review.

As part of this review, produce step-by-step maps for every process your business undertakes. You'll be surprised at what you question.

In this chapter I will introduce you to some of my favourite tried and tested systems and give you an insight into why they are so effective.

Hardware

I have only just stopped stroking the beautiful piece of kit that I bought last year. The man in John Lewis showed me a Macbook Pro and a Macbook Air – "these are the same price" he informed me, "the Air has significantly less storage and no DVD drive", he continued to point out various other reasons why I should buy the Pro over the Air, but I wasn't really listening by this point. "...so it's a no brainer really", he concluded, "you get significantly more for your money with the Macbook Pro".

"I'll take the Air" I said decisively. I was in love.

A highly portable option, perfect for working between home and office. And very *very* sexy. As with a lifelong partner and soul mate, our bond grew stronger and deeper. Every relationship has challenges but we were strong enough to overcome the storage and the DVD issues.

When I bought that machine I had no idea what impact it would have on my productivity. Once a Mac, you'll never go back.

In all seriousness, an investment in efficient hardware is worth every penny of the rewards you'll reap from the surge in your productivity. Likewise, the investment of the time it takes to transfer to new hardware and get to know the tips and tricks to make you work more efficiently is absolutely worth it in the longer term.

Software

I spent probably the best part of six months of what can only be described as pain – researching and choosing the 'right' software, implementing it, realising it wasn't what it said on the tin, going back to the drawing board, finding the right software all over again, going through the process of transferring it over from one system to the next and all the administrative nightmare that goes with that. Documenting processes, getting my team up to speed... the list goes on.

Boy, am I glad I did that now. I can look back and say with confidence that it was the best thing I ever did for my businesses. The pain was worth it. My businesses are now scalable, the processes are slicker and overall our clients experience a more professional service.

Calendar

Use an online calendar so that as your business scales up, you can simply give access to a VA or PA to manage this for you - with ease. It also means that you can access your calendar on the go, book meetings in there and then. You can access it anywhere and it syncs with your phone.

I would strongly recommend Google Calendar. Especially if you are going to be using Gmail.

I'd suggest not having a hardcopy calendar as well as this can be time-consuming to update both and inefficient if someone updates one but not the other. Get your family on board with an online calendar and make it easy for them to access.

Use your online calendar for meetings, appointments, social events and regular time you need to block out (for example for marketing and strategy time). I would generally advise not to use it for To-Do items, unless you have a pressing deadline that you need to set aside time for.

You can also use it for recurring appointments and meetings. I personally use it to put the children's activities, school holidays and social events on too. For me personally, these are relevant as whether my kids have netball or football on that evening, makes a difference to what time I finish working.

If you do choose Google Calendar, here are some handy tips:

Keyboard shortcuts:

S   Takes you to the 'Settings' menu

D   Displays calendar by Day

W   Displays calendar by Week

M   Displays calendar by Month

/   Pulls up the search box

Q   Brings up the 'Quick add' field

If you often join webinars hosted in a different time zone, you can get Google Calendar to display multiple timezones. From the 'Settings' menu, go to the 'General' tab and click 'Show an additional time zone' and then tick the box 'Display all time zones'.

You can also add National Holidays. To activate this, from the 'Settings' menu, click on the 'Calendars' tab, then 'Browse interesting calendars'. You can now preview and subscribe to various calendars.

Your calendar works in conjunction with your To-Do list. As a general rule your calendar tells you *where* you need to be and your To-Do list tells you *what* you need to do. With the exception of your daily implementation hour, there shouldn't be much of an overlap between the two.

Dictation Software

Although you may find it pretty em-barr-ass-in-g tooo taaal-k liiii-ke th-iiiii-s (full stop, new paragraph), Dragon Dictate is a quick way to send texts and emails. You will need to get used to how to sp-eeeea-k tooo i-t but once you've got the hang of it you can dictate texts and emails. It's not quite 'there' yet in terms of being able to transcribe lengthier dictations such as blogs and reports, but for shorter dictations it's not bad.

Be careful if doing this in a public place; you may get cautioned for odd behaviour.

Don't get too excited before you have tried it. It's far from perfect. When I got home one day to read "Buy sparkle turd" on my To-Do list, it took me a while to realise that it should say "Pay Barclaycard". **Dragon Dictate** and I have taken a while to get to know each other. We have an up and down relationship. But we've had some laughs along the way.

To Do List

You need to find a To-Do list App to suit you personally. There are hundreds of them out there. As an obsessive organiser, I've researched and tested pretty much all of the main ones. I keep my ears to the ground and gather that Evernote is pretty popular.

Personally, I keep coming back time and again to '**ToDo Cloud**' by Appigo. I have it on my iPhone and iPad and Macbook. They all sync perfectly and I've never had any problems to date.

5 reasons why 'ToDo' by Appigo is effective:

1. Seamless Sync

It seamlessly syncs across my phone, tablet and laptop, making it easy to update on any of these devices – which I regularly do – throughout the day. I hope I'm not tempting fate here but I've never experienced a synching issue in the years I've been using it.

2. Focus

The 'Focus' feature means you only focus on what's important today. You can set the parameters for this – mine is all tasks overdue + tasks due today. Not having the whole of your rather large To-Do list staring you in the face takes the overwhelm out of the day and keeps that emphasis on immediately due tasks only.

3. Categorisation

I'm an advocate of grouping tasks (or time blocking) to heighten productivity. This means making all of your calls in one go for example, checking & sending emails in one block, putting aside any errands that take you away from your desk and doing them together. To Do allows you to assign a category to tasks, which can be a great help when grouping tasks.

4. Simplicity

Visually it's great. The iPad app is an interesting design – a bit like a Filofax (but in a good way). It attracts a lot of interest from intrigued colleagues and everyone who has seen it wants it! The iPhone version is a simple design too, and perfectly ample. To-Do is overall an easy to use, intuitive App.

5. Customisable

Whilst the custom settings are fine, the thing I love about To Do is that is allows you to design how your list is built and presented. You can add Notes to support tasks (web links, email addresses, copy & paste emails or texts into there). You can also choose the way things are crossed off – a neat line, a tick, a strikethrough. An important choice to make – this contributes to that great satisfied feeling you get when ticking something off. Ah, the little things!

Finance & Accounting

If you are still producing your invoices manually on Excel or Word, there is an easier way and it's time to change.

FRESHBOOKS

Do you manage a team of people (whether that is contractors or employees)? If you do, you may want to consider using Freshbooks. Your team individually update their hours or project milestones and it instantly updates onto your Freshbooks account.

My favourite timesaver with Freshbooks is the clever function which pulls in time and projects worked for a client from all contractors that have been involved and automatically produces and emails an invoice to the client. Hey presto! That's a great example of how I have significantly cut down the time spent on collating everyone's invoices and timesheets, which came in various formats. With a team of over 20 contractors, quite frankly it was an administrative nightmare before I discovered Freshbooks.

It's my understanding from research that very few cloud accounting systems offer this function. **Clearbooks** is another who does.

Freshbooks as a company are a delight to deal with. From a customer experience perspective, they ooze simplicity and efficiency. And we love nothing more than working with like-minded companies who display these traits. From the look and feel of their website through to the friendly customer service, we've been a very happy client of theirs for quite some time now.

As with all software, we stay on our toes and are never complacent or naive enough to think that it's always going to be the best on the market. We've not found better yet, although Clearbooks does come close for us.

XERO

Xero Accounting is cloud-based software that can dovetail with Freshbooks with a feed if you choose to use these two systems together.

It enables direct bank feeds, real-time collaboration, smart reports and a financial dashboard. With no upfront costs or installation and online training and support, Xero is an ideal alternative to desktop based software if you need access anywhere or if your bookkeeping is done for you and you need real time access to your business numbers.

If you don't have a team whose time needs to be fed straight into your client invoices, then you could use Xero for everything, including invoicing and use of Freshbooks isn't really necessary.

If you bank with HSBC you're onto a winner. You can set up a direct daily feed to come from your bank account straight into Xero, rather than having to manually upload it, which (at the time of writing this) you have to do for all other UK banks.

It's an active market out there for cloud accounting software, with plenty of competition and upcoming businesses fighting for a piece of the action. Xero appears to be one of the most popular for small businesses currently, but the way things are going that could potentially change in the near future.

Know your Business Numbers

Do you waste a countless amount of time staring blankly at your accounts figures? Wondering exactly what they mean, how to convert them?

Find yourself a really good accountant. By really good, I mean an accountant who treats you and your business individually. He or she will get to understand your business and produce the important numbers that you need to know.

After years of frustration with having to fathom out inflexible Sage reports that made no sense, and only having annual communication with my accountant (and that was by email to hand them my year-end figures on a plate), I met the most refreshing chartered accountant ever.

He told me which numbers I needed to know and how to calculate them. He talked about numbers that *really* mattered to a small business – apart from the obvious P&L, etc. he talked to me about needing to understand the cost of converting leads, a customer lifetime value, my break-even point, how profitable customers are, controlling costs, budgeting for tax, considering credit-worthiness of clients and monitoring cash flow.

Everything suddenly made perfect sense, I understood what I *really* needed to know. Needless to say, he is now my accountant and we worked together to find the best accounting system (rather than him telling me I had to go with what he uses). He has written an e-book about knowing your business numbers, of which he over-generously credits me as co-author - *Figure It Out* by Noel Guilford.

Project Management Software

To keep a track of where you are up to with multiple projects that you have on the go simultaneously, you need to find a system that works well for you. Otherwise you can easily lose track of where everything is up to. Whilst your To-Do list can help, it's just not the same as purpose-built project management software.

There are some good tools out there to use for this. The benefits and appeal vary depending on requirements. Some are free, some paid for. There's plenty of choice.

With running more than one business and working with numerous contractors, I have plenty of projects to manage. **Basecamp** ticked most boxes for me as it's great for collaborative working and I got excited when I first started using it. I thought it was 'the one'. Unfortunately it let me down on one basic project management function - I was staggered that there wasn't an option to produce a report to show all overdue tasks. Such a shame as other than that it was perfect in every way.

During our journey to find the best software for our needs, we came across and tested **Asana** and **Trello** – both popular options amongst owners of growing small businesses. Other recommendations from the entrepreneurs we asked were **TeamworkPM** and **Liquid Planner**.

Email Marketing Software

There are lots of features of email marketing software that we love from a time-efficiency point of view.

One being that you can automate emails to your mailing list every time you post to your blog. Another is that you can set up auto-responders for people who sign up to your newsletter, which effectively automates part of your marketing process, keeping you firmly in the forefront of that potential client's mind.

We moved from **Mailchimp** to **Aweber** so I'm familiar with both. Both are decent with similar functionality, but we took a longer-term view when we chose Aweber. It's intuitive to use, you can choose between single or double opt-in and it generally appeared more flexible than Mailchimp for our particular needs.

Infusionsoft – affectionately referred to as Confusionsoft - is king. This is a step up from Mailchimp or Aweber. And so is the price. When you make that leap, just make sure you have a good expert on hand who understands it, or that you are willing to invest a lot of time (and money in training) to learn it yourself.

Social Media Engagement

There aren't many businesses that *wouldn't* benefit from hopping on the social media bus. It's time-consuming to keep on top of it, but it can create some great business opportunities. So, once you've narrowed it down to the channels that work for your business, try streamlining your involvement.

Use software such as **Hootsuite** to update multiple social media channels together. There are conflicting views on whether updating multiple channels with the same content is good practice or not, and it may vary from business to business. The principal rule if you are updating multiple channels is to make sure you choose updates that are suitable for all platforms.

Set aside a period of time regularly to think up some social media updates (include some subtle sales in there but not too much). This should be updates that are not time-bound, such as offers, quotes and timeless or undated articles. Then schedule these to go out as far in advance as you want.

Spend a little time researching good quality blogs and newsworthy sites that provide information that your clients and potential clients will be interested in. Put yourself in the shoes of your clients – what would you want to hear about? For Vi-VA's clients it's tips on how to save time or do something more efficiently, any new cutting edge software, exciting technology updates and generally anything that covers business growth. What are your clients interested in?

Sign up to the RSS feeds for these sites and on a regular basis (preferably daily), check out your feed reader, scan the articles and pick out interesting information to post to social media. Always offer an opinion, preferably provocative, to stimulate engagement.

In terms of on-going engagement, it's important that you understand which channels are the most effective for your business and focus on only these. You can waste hours and hours of time engaging on numerous different social media platforms. Don't get me wrong, if that is an effective use of your time and it brings in business, go right ahead. But dare I suggest that a lot of this time spent is wasted, and could be concentrated into one or two channels, saving a lot of time.

If you write a blog (and you should), consider outsourcing some or all of this.

Online Filing

Try a 'cloud' storage system to keep everything - documents, photos, videos, music - in one place. You can access it from anywhere and it saves wasting time searching for lost files across computers and duplication of files.

There are plenty of options out there including **Amazon Cloud Drive** and **LiveDrive**. One of our favourites is **Dropbox**.

The great thing about Dropbox is that you can install the desktop app and it seamlessly synchronises with 'the cloud'. If you use more than one machine, you can install the Dropbox desktop app on each machine. On your computer, Dropbox looks just like any other folder on there – you can save to it and drag & drop files into it.

You can also share individual files and folders within your Dropbox folder with people so their computers will have exactly the same things on as yours. This is great for collaborating with teams and particularly with sharing large files.

Reassess your bookmarked sites (or 'favourites'). Do you still use them? Are they still appropriate to you? Which sites do you visit all of the time? Make a list of them and make sure they are all bookmarked so you can access them quickly.

You may want to include:

- Your email (if you use webmail / Gmail)
- Your To-Do List
- Social Media sites
- Online Banking
- Your Invoicing Software
- Your CRM System
- The store you buy your printer cartridges from
- Business blogs you visit regularly
- Your own website (should be visited regularly)
- Resource sites you visit
- Client websites

Apps

Of course there is an App for pretty much everything now.

Most of the software systems I've talked about so far in this chapter has an App – Google Calendar, Dragon Dictate, To Do, Freshbooks, Xero, Facebook, Twitter, LinkedIn, Google+, Hootsuite, Asana, Basecamp, Trello, Basecamp, Mailchimp, Dropbox.

And there's an App for all the other time-consuming tasks to make your life easier – online banking, QR code readers, mind mapping and lots more.

IT Support

How fast and reliable is your broadband? Depending on what business you are in, will depend on how critical is that you have superfast broadband. With my business for example, clients are paying by the hour and certainly don't want to be paying for our time twiddling our thumbs whilst the internet slowly whirs into action. They expect instant high-speed connection and rightly so.

Are you on a home package or a business package? Business lines will receive priority if things go wrong. And if they go down for a period of time you may be able to claim compensation towards loss of earnings. Sometimes it's worth paying a bit extra for peace of mind.

What happens when your emails go down? When you have software or hardware problems that you're inexperienced in dealing with? When you're working on a client deadline and technology goes wrong and prevents you from meeting it?

Build a relationship with an IT company. They don't necessarily have to be local, as long as they are reputable, they should be able to resolve most issues through remotely accessing your computer. There are affordable monthly retainer packages available for small businesses where you can call for help if things do go wrong.

It's advisable in business to have MS Office and to always keep up to date with the latest version. Again, you can rent this from an IT company for a nominal monthly fee – it actually works out to be a similar amount to buying it from new every time a new version is released.

"My time has value. Therefore, it is crucial that I spend my time focused on those things that are the best use of my time and deliver the most effective results. Anything that is not the best use of my time I delegate"
Alan Sugar

CHAPTER 8
Virtual Assistants

Why you should use a VA / Bookkeeper

Many entrepreneurs are avid fans of using Virtual Assistants (or VAs) as they realise the benefits. Nigel Botterill – the entrepreneurial marmite - is one of them. The straight-talking Yorkshire man tells it as it is:

"If you are a business owner and you do your own book-keeping then either you are certifiably insane, OR, lacking in all ambition to grow, OR, unenlightened. Most small businesses will find that their book- keeping only takes 3 - 4 hours per month IF an experienced, qualified book-keeper is doing the work. Therefore

if you remove book-keeping from your list of things to do this will free up probably at least five or six hours of your time per month – plus a whole load of mental baggage that you've been carrying around with you whilst you've been worrying about having to do your book-keeping.

You can get a heck of a lot of marketing done in six hours. You can see a heck of a lot of potential new customers in six hours. If you spend six hours working "on" your business rather than 'in' your business and you do that regularly month on month, your business will be transformed by Christmas.

In short, it's like having your own team of employees behind you – but without the expense. This enables you to fulfil your business aspirations in a practical and cost-effective way.

They not only free up a lot of your time, and are incredibly cost-effective, but the third reason why you ought to use a VA in your business is because of the flexibility. They're here to help your business as and when you need them. Some weeks I've used VAs for as much as forty hours' work in a week – others I've had no support at all. It's like a tap. I just turn it on and off as and when I need it. It really is brilliant."

Unsure About Going Virtual?

Most of us have been used to dealing with people face-to-face, but increasingly we're interacting with others virtually. Meetings are being replaced with Skype, Vidyo, FaceTime, Google Hangouts and other technology. With increased home working, teams are collaborating through cloud-based software and smartphone apps. Social media means easy communication with friends and colleagues across the globe. It's no different working with a Virtual Assistant – only they can't make your tea or coffee!

When you eliminate the need for personal proximity it opens the doors to tremendous opportunities. This enables your VA team to source the best-matched individual VA to your needs, regardless of their location geographically.

How Can I Monitor The Work Being Done by my VA?

You could ask this of anyone you have working for you, whether virtual or not. In fact, your VA is more accountable to you than most permanent employees. Apart from seeing the results your VA will achieve, as a way of evaluating performance, they should complete timesheets recording all the tasks undertaken and the time each took, so you can audit the time worked by task and date. It's in the interest of a Virtual Assistant to do a top job, in order to keep you as a repeat client. A good VA will put themselves in your shoes and flag when they feel that a task you've asked them to do isn't a cost-effective exercise.

What Would I Get A VA To-do?

I'm constantly asked "What would I get a VA To-do?" or "What do you do for your other clients?" We all know the top three or four activities we do best – so write those down. These will include the activities you do that add the most value to your organisation. Everything not on this list (and we know how many things you actually have To-do to run your own business) is a task that your VA can undertake. Some of the most common things VAs are asked to do include: follow-up sales and marketing calls, diary management & meeting booking, travel booking and itinerary, newsletter distribution, invoice raising and chasing, bookkeeping, spreadsheet design and social media updates & interaction.

Research is another time consumer that you can delegate to your VA - whether it's products, best deals, information for presentations or blog posts, best priced travel deals.

By delegating tasks to a VA you stay focused on what you do best, and ultimately grow your bottom line.

How Does a VA Keep Connected with Me?

So many of the relationships we have are virtual; an Assistant needn't be any different. If you think about large corporate companies, they are virtual in many ways – sales people on the road, departments in other buildings and even entire divisions in other cities or countries. Your VA is just like that.

To make sure your VA stays connected, you can schedule a regular phone call to make sure you are working from the same page. If you prefer a more face-to-face approach you can use Skype regularly or even arrange a meeting every quarter. Your VA can be part of your team updates / Skype meetings so that you will forget, in fact, that they are virtual at all.

I'm Unsure About Committing to a VA Before I've Tried One Out

Look at a few options – VAs have strengths in different areas. Decide on whether you need a small 'one man band' VA or access to a wider range of skills by working with a multi-VA business. Favour recommended VAs – ask around in your business circles, put a question out there on LinkedIn. Speak to a VA at length before you commit, after all you will need to gel with them and have similar business principles.

We like to test-drive a car, have a 30-day free trial of a new app, hear a snippet of a song before we buy. Similarly with some VAs you can have a free trial with no obligation.

How Many Hours Will I Need from a VA?

It's difficult to estimate this, and you won't know how long something will take until you have determined what you want your VA to do. The best place to start is to take a moment to write down all the tasks you would ideally like to delegate. Then estimate how long it takes you to do each of these tasks. The good news is, it probably won't take your VA as long as it takes you – once they are trained up to how you work - they may well surprise you with their efficiency.

A lot of VAs work on a retainer basis or a minimum number of hours per month. This may or may not suit you – you may want to check before you sign up.

How Do I Control Costs?

VAs work in different ways when it comes to charging. You may receive a discount for buying hours in bulk and paying for them upfront or going onto a retainer package. It's important that the payment plan you choose will not restrict you or your business in any way. The beauty of Virtual Assistance is supposed to be its flexibility, so keep this in the forefront of your mind.

How Do You Get Your VA To Book a Trip You Will Enjoy?

Naturally, you want to make sure that your VA is going to book and plan a business trip that meets your needs. This is why it is a good idea to make sure you give your VA an opportunity to get to know you.

The more your VA knows about you, the easier it will be for them to book a hotel and transportation that meets your needs. One easy solution is to create a list of what amenities you need a hotel to offer. And advise your preferences for train travel for example (forward-facing, power required, whether minimum changes or overall journey time is more important). You should also create a list of what types of food you prefer to eat. This way your VA can book a room in a hotel that is within a reasonable distance of restaurants that you are willing to dine at. You'll only have to tell a good VA this information once and they should bear it in mind with all future travel arrangements from that point onwards.

Virtual Assistant vs. Employee – The Real Costs will shock you

Thinking of taking on an employee? You may want to think again.

The only reason to employ people in your business is if you can make more profit by doing so than doing everything yourself or outsourcing. And the only people you should employ are profitable ones.

That said, how do you know which of your employees are profitable? Unfortunately you don't unless you know how

142

much they cost, and I mean *really* cost. You see most businesses only calculate a proportion of the cost of employing someone. It goes something like: wages + benefits + employer's national insurance + overheads. Some neglect overheads, but then employees take up space, require heat and light, drink tea and use stationery and the bathroom so you need to take into account space, utilities and supplies.

So an employee paid £10 per hour, plus a Christmas party, bonus and national insurance may actually cost, say £12 per hour. If it costs £2,400 per month for overheads and you employ 4 people, that is £600 each, divided by 150 work hours is £4 per hour, so we are already up to £16 per hour.

But there is more. The real cost of employing people includes three more elements which hardly any businesses take in to account:

The first is rework and the cost of mistakes. Even if you have great, documented systems which specify exactly how a job should be done (and most businesses don't) your employees will make defective goods, ship them to the wrong place, pack them poorly, waste materials, not answer the phone, fail to follow up leads and a host of other mistakes that cost you business and money. And 100% of these errors is your cost. The amount obviously varies by business and employee but conservatively will be at least £300 – £400 per week per employee, so that's another £10 per hour making £26 per hour.

Next is the cost of absenteeism and its partner presenteeism (being present but not actually making you money). Absenteeism is easy to calculate: it is holidays, personal and sick leave, training days and so on. Presenteeism is harder to calculate but it is there just the same. It is the time spent on personal phone calls and emails, surfing the internet, researching holiday destinations, chatting to colleagues, reading a book or magazine, taking a smoke break or just doing nothing. Left unsupervised, this time can be significant. If only a third of the time you pay for is wasted (and some studies suggest it is far more than that) then that means your hourly cost will increase to £39 per hour.

The last element of employee cost that is often overlooked is your time. In big businesses this cost is easy to calculate because it's the cost of HR departments and middle managers, but in most small businesses it is your time. You are leader, manager and supervisor, you have to recruit, train, appraise and sometimes fire. Let's assume your time is worth £100 per hour and each employee takes up 2 hours of your time per week, that's another £5 per hour making a total of £44 per hour. Did you realise that was how much you were paying your staff?

The final calculation you need to do is to work out how much profit your employees need to make to ensure that investment is worthwhile. In other words what is their return on investment? At £44 per hour, that is £6,500 per month or £79,000 a year per employee! What level of profit do you need to justify that amount of investment?

The cost of employing people is often the single biggest, and least understood, cost in most small businesses and is often 'hidden' because the accounts only show the wages + benefits + employer's national insurance element. If you really want to understand your business numbers, and use them to drive strategies such as outsourcing, then you need to understand the real cost of employing your staff.

The Answer?

Use a Virtual Assistant. They are target-driven as they're only as good as their satisfied clients. They won't be chatting round the coffee machine, making personal calls in your time or leaving early when you're not in the office. And they are a heck of a lot cheaper, even though it may not seem that way at first glance. You have now been armed with information that will help you decide the real cost of outsourcing v employing.

"Focusing is about saying No"
Steve Jobs

CHAPTER 9
Dealing with Distractions

"It's Urgent!"

Really? OK, taking away all the obvious emergency situations (someone is dying, in danger, etc.), what situations in a business situation *are* actually urgent?

I would suggest very few. Unless you work in the city as a trader.

Don't be bamboozled into dealing with tasks by how loud someone shouts or how many times they call or email. The neurotic box-tickers who have an overwhelming compulsion to get something ticked off their own To-Do list and out of their head-space are a classic example of people who unreasonably class something as urgent. It's only urgent in *their* head. This is *their* problem, not yours.

These are the people who call as well as email about the same thing, people who text you a second time if you don't reply within an hour, call you repeatedly until you answer. This alone can cause enough pressure for you to want to just deal with the task there and then, just to get them off your back. But don't. Otherwise they'll do it again. And again. You need to educate these people that you never jump unless you believe it is *positively* urgent.

Get to recognise who these people are. As you are reading this, you may be smiling, already thinking of someone you know who fits the description.

Question any deadline that doesn't seem realistic or essential: *"I can certainly do [task] for you. I won't be able to meet your deadline of X. I can however, get it done for Y".*

Make your boundaries clear to those around you

Tell your family and friends when you are not available to take their calls or unplanned visits.

If you work from home, some people think it's fine to rock up uninvited and unannounced. I have been in mid flow of a crucial conversation with a client before now, when my doorbell has been rang repeatedly. When I ignored it, the person in question decided to let themselves into my back garden and start banging on the window of the room I was sat in! Not exactly conducive to a focused, professional conversation to close a sale with a potential client.

Taking uninterrupted time out

When you are constantly surrounded by white noise you can easily fail to remember what's important and begin to lose your way. You need time out to reflect and to give yourself time in a different environment away from the hustle and bustle and the white noise.

This allows you to take a step back, a step outside of the day-to-day running of your business, and realise what is going well and what may need some attention or tweaking.

Find a place where you feel calm, at ease and inspired. That place could be anywhere – overlooking the sea… a pub in the country… people watching from a café… in a garden. It's very personal to you. Try to go to that special place at least once every week, even just for a few hours. For those few hours, don't give yourself the pressure of any deadlines, just work at a leisurely place – preferably on the strategy of your business. With your phone and emails switched off, lose yourself in that time. Enjoy it thoroughly and appreciate the release from the white noise.

During this time, you'll find that new ideas will flow, realisations will materialise. You'll return to your office motivated and focused, the knock-on impact being increased productivity.

Decide on a set day for this and put time aside for it every week. Block it out in your calendar. Let your clients, your team and your suppliers know that you don't work on, let's say Thursday afternoons. Stick to this. Don't answer your mobile or emails during this time. Be uncontactable every single Thursday afternoon. Train people to realise this; it will take less time than you think. Don't feel the need to explain why. Just be polite but firm about it:

"I won't be available on Thursday afternoons from next week. If you have an urgent query during this time, you can contact my VA Antonia on antonia@vi-va.co.uk or call XXXX. She will be happy to help if she can".

You can even record a similar message and have it as your voicemail for that afternoon only.

And then there's your Daily Implementation Time. Exactly the same applies - this time should be uninterrupted. As with your time-out, communicate to everyone you need to that you are not to be disturbed.

Call Answering

I was very excited to receive a call from a 'Dragon' recently. I'm not talking a scary woman here, I'm talking a celebrity entrepreneur, famous for appearing on the TV show 'Dragon's Den' on BBC2. Here's the main gist of her voicemail to me:

"Hi Sarah... Sue recommended you highly, although I have to say it's a concern if I get your answer machine. I need someone who can act as my VA who would respond when I needed them...."

Oops. If that wasn't a trigger to start using a call answering service...

So I did. And I can highly recommend it. For an affordable monthly cost you can have your calls answered professionally and consistently, without interruption to you. Some call answering services will also take on basic tasks such as diary management. It's also a great excuse to stop non-urgent calls from family and friends during working hours – explain to them you are charged by the call answering service for every call received. That seems to stop them.

Aside from the fact that you never have to answer your phone again, and you are no longer interrupted when you're trying to focus, apparently 80% of people who get through to a voicemail hang up. I think there's a few good reasons there to at least trial a call answering service as a professional front to your business.

Interruptions on your Mobile

And just in case friends and family think that your mobile is an acceptable way of contacting you, make it clear that it isn't. If you do receive calls on your mobile, a great trick is to sound busy - as if you are dashing into a meeting or to an appointment (even if you're not!) If you speak with a sense of urgency, often this technique is quicker than letting voicemail take the call, which just adds another item to your To-Do list ('Call Gareth back'):

"Sorry Lucy, I'm just working on a deadline/going to a meeting. I do want to speak to you. Would you mind calling back after 5pm when I can give you my full attention?"

Note that you put the ball firmly back in their court to call you.

And sometimes just switch it off. Yes, really.

Stopping Unwanted Sales Calls

Whether you decide to use a call answering service or not, you still need to put a stop to those pesky sales calls. You don't want to have to deal with them yourself and you certainly don't want to have to pay your call answering service to deal with them.

So how do you stop them?

First and foremost, register with the Telephone Preference Service (TPS) or the Corporate Telephone Preference Service (CTPS). These are central opt out registers where individuals and businesses can register their wish not to receive unsolicited sales and marketing telephone calls. It's a legal requirement that companies do not make such calls to numbers registered on the TPS and CTPS.

Register with the TPS if you are a consumer at your residential address, a sole trader or, except in Scotland, a partnership. Register with the CTPS to register a corporate business (limited company, public limited company and Scottish partnership) or organisation. Registering is free, quick and simple to do. It is funded by the direct marketing industry. You can register here at http://www.tpsonline.org.uk/.

If you don't have a call answering service, I would recommend that you don't answer 'blocked', 'unknown' or 'out of area' phone calls – this should sift out most of the sales calls. If you get caught out and unknowingly answer a sales call, here are some responses that we find work well:

Can I speak to Mr/Mrs XXX please?

"No sorry, she moved out a long time ago."

Are you the home owner?

"No, it's rented."

Are you the business owner?

"No, they live abroad and are not contactable."

Did you know you are entitled to free loft / cavity wall insulation?

"I don't own the property."

Did you know you are entitled to a PPI refund from your bank?

"I've never had PPI in my life, so I definitely am not. But thank you for thinking of me." [click]

If all else fails:

"Someone's at the door, got to run". [click]

or

"Someone's calling my other line, I'm expecting an urgent call. Sorry, bye". [click]

or

"I'm expecting an urgent call. I have to keep this line free. I'm sorry, bye". [click]

Or the one that works the best:

"Can I ask where you got my number? I'm registered with the Telephone Preference Service, which means that you calling me is against the law."

This time the hang up click is not at your end!

Text or email instead of calling

If you really do miss a call, consider texting that person back in response to their voicemail, to save getting into a lengthy discussion: for example: "Thx for your voicemail, sorry I can't do Thurs, I've pencilled in Fri at 10, any good for you?" Always anticipate the response and answer it – in this example you are doing this by suggesting an alternative time.

The same applies if you need to contact someone. Can it be done by text (or email)?

If you have a Mac, Macbook or iPad, you can text (iMessage) from there. The recipient has to have an Apple device too of course, but a lot of people do have nowadays. I 'text' from my Macbook Air all the time and love it. It takes seconds, rather than sending clumsy time-consuming texts from my iPhone.

If someone doesn't have an Apple device, then you need to suggest they buy one to make your life easier. I'm joking of course. Well only slightly. There is another simple way to text non-Apple users if you, like me, are a 'sausage-finger' texter, and that is via your To-Do list App.

OK, so start by typing a text straight onto your To-Do list from your computer. This will sync instantly with the To-Do App on your phone, where you can simply copy it and paste it into a text message.

Sound like a faff? It may be for the first couple of times, but once you get used to it, it will honestly save you time. But the best is yet to come…

You can also use this technique for following things up in the future. For example, one of my team told me on Friday that she had a meeting with a potential new client booked for the following Wednesday. There and then I typed onto my To-Do list the following:

"Hi Rachael, How did the meeting with Alex go today?" and allocated a date of next Wednesday. When next Wednesday comes, I simply copy & paste this from the To-Do list on my phone straight onto a text and hit send. Done.

Phone Tag

A frustrating waste of time is playing phone tag. If you find yourself in this situation, try to answer the query on that person's voicemail or if they don't say why they are calling, pre-empt what they may want and respond accordingly on voicemail.

For example, you asked Joe Jones to call back in a month when you have clearer plans for your new project. He calls a month later and you miss his call. You can pretty much assume he's calling for an update – so when you call him back leave the update on his voicemail. Nip it in the bud to prevent yet another missed call. Alternatively, email or text the update.

Return calls only twice a day. Or better still, get your VA to do this for you.

Distractions from Staff

Note what distractions you are getting from people you work with and whether they could be prevented. Can you empower people so they can make decisions without your input? Do they need more training in order to deal with certain tasks? For every interruption, consciously consider what you can do to stop that distraction happening in future.

You may want to allocate a set time for catching up with your staff on non-urgent queries - an 'open door' policy for an hour where they can come to talk to you (or call you if you work virtually). Make it clear to them what this time is for and educate them to use it wisely. Make sure you are committed to being fully available during this time, or it won't work. Putting this structure in place will make everyone more productive.

If you have an office, stand up when people come in. And stay standing. People are much less likely to pull up a chair and take a seat if you are standing. You may want to even put some paperwork or files on any available chairs, so that there is nowhere to sit, even if people are cheeky enough to try. As soon as you've answered their question, walk to the door and politely hold it for them as a subtle hint to hurry them out.

Set Expectations

Set the expectation of anyone you work with, particularly those who are sensitive, that your emails, texts and phone calls sometimes need to be quick and therefore will be to the point and contain no fluff. If they are professional, they should understand and accept this willingly (if they don't then you may want to question why you are working with them). This may seem harsh, but I'm not asking you to be rude here, I'm simply asking you to lay ground rules for the way you sometimes need to communicate as an efficient, busy professional.

You should also set expectations about how you need people working with you to be easily contactable and if they are unavailable how soon you would expect them to get back to you. As long as you don't expect them to reply immediately at weekends and be at the end of a phone in the evenings, this is not an unreasonable request. It will save you time hanging around waiting for tardy text and email replies. Everyone knows where they stand. If people don't want to work with you, you are not forcing them to.

Beat those Bad Habits

Emails and social media are the two primary culprits for distracting people during their working day. It's no wonder so many large companies block social media and webmail sites and ban their staff from using them during work time.

As a small business owner, these are two necessary components of your business, so it's impossible to avoid them during your working day. You can however take steps to reduce the temptation and limit the time you spend on them. This can take real willpower, especially for compulsive email checkers, of whom there are plenty.

We've already covered the tricks to this, but as a reminder:

- Make sure email notifications are turned off
- Check emails twice each day (at set times) and no more
- For any emails you need to send, save them for your set email time
- Close down your email client and only open it twice a day for checking
- Keep off social media completely unless you are actively engaging for business purposes

For home workers, another culprit of disruption to your working day is Domestic Distractions (or as I call them, DDs). I'm talking about hanging out washing, sorting out leftover breakfast dishes and essentially anything else visible that you can potter round doing rather than working. It's called procrastination.

Factor in a 5 minute whirlwind tidy before you start work. And if you're not able to do that, treat these distractions as if they are invisible. Learn to ignore them - let them wait until later, just as they would if you had run out of the door this morning to go to an office.

Day not going as Planned?

You have planned your day's activities with precision. You've had a great start to the day, everything is on track and things are going well.

At 11:30am the phone rings. It's a potential new client who has many questions; this is going to be a long call. You have to be at a meeting with an existing client in an hour. Before then you have to get a task back to a client that you need to check over. A text comes in whilst you're on the phone, it's from your partner who now has to work late and can't collect the kids from school. You need to email a quote to the potential client following your call. They've asked for it today. Four other voicemails have come in to your mobile whilst you've been on the landline: your business partner needs to speak to you about a great new opportunity, one of your team has called in sick and is due with a client in 2 hours time, your sister has called sounding upset asking for you to call her back as soon as possible and a friend has asked if you can recommend a good plumber.

One of the main items already on your To-Do list for today was preparation for tomorrow afternoon's strategy planning session. You need to call the Doctor's before 5pm, as you've been putting this off for a few days now. You have a vague nagging feeling that you promised to get back to someone about something - you know it stemmed from yesterday but you just can't remember who and what. But you know they're expecting you to get back to them and you don't want to let them down.

This may well be a typical day for you. It reiterates why you should never have more than 10 items on your To-Do list in one day.

It's very easy to panic in this situation and to drop everything already on your To-Do list to deal with these seemingly urgent requests. But Don't! Otherwise you will spend your life fire-fighting and your business will drown. Instead, take a deep breath, a step back and apply the **GIFOD** principle. I'll show you how.

To summarise, here are the 7 extra items that you now need to deal with:

1. Check task for client and send by email
2. Rearrange day to collect children from school
3. Email potential new client with quote
4. Speak to business partner re new opportunity
5. Arrange for replacement team member to visit client
6. Call sister back
7. Recommend a plumber

So you've taken a step back, a deep breath and you've made the wise choice not to panic. You now need to make a swift and crude prioritisation. For each task ask yourself:

Can I do it in a few minutes?

If yes, do it.

If no, apply the **GIFOD** principle:

G   Goals - Is it in line with my goals?

I   Impact - Will anyone be in danger or seriously upset if I don't do it?

F   Financial - Will I lose money by not doing it?

O   Outsource - Can it be outsourced? (to a VA)

D   Defer - Can it be deferred?

Taking each task in turn, firstly ask yourself: **Can I do it in a few minutes?**

1. Check task for client and send by email

    MAYBE. But assuming it's not a small task, probably not.

    Apply GIFOD.

2. Rearrange day to collect children from school

    POSSIBLY. Your children are a priority. Who is the meeting with? If it's with a client, do you have someone you can call on to collect your children? If you do, send a quick text or make a quick call.

    If they can't help, is there anyone else you can send to the meeting in your absence? Again, send a quick call or text.

    If it's not with a client, send a quick text, apologise and explain something unexpected has come up.

    This is one that can genuinely be categorised as 'urgent' and should be on your radar (and in your head space) until it's been sorted.

    NB: If you cancel meetings on a regular basis, you will lose credibility. If you only do it when it's unavoidable, people will understand. Make a note to speak to your partner later about whether the situation could have been avoided. Have a backup person in place for picking up the children in this situation ever arises in the future – a parent, sibling or friend, for example.

3. Email potential new client with quote

   UNLIKELY, *assuming a bespoke quote is required. It pays to put effort into this to make sure you get the work.*

   Apply GIFOD.

4. Speak to business partner re new opportunity

   YES. *Pick up the phone. Explain quickly to your business partner that you're having a busy day and you only have a couple of minutes. Ask them to condense it down. If it requires another conversation, establish the importance (i.e. is it time sensitive) then schedule a time there and then to continue the conversation and put it on your To-do list. Done.*

5. Arrange for replacement team member to visit client

   POTENTIALLY. *You can certainly get a quick call in to the client to explain and start the ball rolling by getting a group text out to your other available options for cover asking for an immediate response.*

6. Call sister back

   DEFINITELY NOT. *You can't rush a family member who is upset.*

   Another urgent one. Hopefully you don't need to apply GIFOD, but I've included it below for the less sensitive reading this.

7. Recommend a plumber

   YES. *Assuming you know one. Act now. Simply forward a contact card from your phone list. Done.*

Now, apply the **GIFOD** Principle:

- Kick out any tasks that are not in line with your **G**oals (i.e. no tick in 1st column)
- Tasks with **I**mpact should be dealt with straight away
- Weigh up the importance of tasks with a **F**inancial implication and make a call on how quickly they need attending to
- Delegate any tasks that can be **O**utsourced to your VA
- Tasks that can be **D**eferred should be put off until at least tomorrow - add them to your To-Do list.

This leaves calling your sister, making sure the school pick-up situation is sorted and checking one of your team can cover the

Task	Goals	Impact	Financial	Outsource	Defer
Check task for client and send by email	✔	✘	✔	✔	✘
Email potential new client with quote	✔	✘	✔	✔	✘
Call sister back	✔	✔	✘	✘	✘

client visit.

You could potentially delegate 2 out of these 3 tasks to your VA, leaving only one additional task for you to deal with today – calling your sister. Suddenly the chaos that you started to experience only half an hour ago has dispersed and all is calm again.

I would suggest that you have the GIFOD template easily accessible in your Organisational Folder or on your phone or tablet, for ease of prioritising. For one task you can apply it easily, but if, as in the example above, four things come in at once, then it can be useful to use it as a tool to dismiss panic and create clarity.

"How do you eat an elephant? Answer: A bite at a time"

Children's riddle, author unknown

CHAPTER 10
Working through Unproductive Periods

Even the most self-motivated business owners can have off days. Especially if you are your own boss and work alone.

Setting Mini Deadlines

If you are someone with an overactive brain and a short attention span who thrives on excitement, change and fresh opportunities, there will be days when you get bored easily. If you have that personality type, you'll know that it can be a struggle to stick with one task for a long period. So how do you stay motivated, particularly if you work from home and you are your own boss? It can certainly take mental stamina at times.

If you've tried every trick in the book to improve your concentration levels and not yet found the perfect solution, let me introduce mini deadlines. It goes against what a lot of time management books suggest, but it can be very effective for certain personality types.

The idea is to break your day up into chunks. And for each chunk to set yourself mini deadlines. This means deliberately going for a walk, having a meeting or introducing a change every couple of hours throughout the day. The short bursts of concentrated time between these breaks will make you more focused than ever. Far more in fact than if a full-uninterrupted day stretched out ahead of you; that's just daunting - a recipe for procrastination.

So why does this quirky way of working get more done than a conventional approach?

It's a day filled with mini goals. Mini meaning entirely within reach. Nothing too overwhelming. Most people work better under pressure, so giving yourself these mini deadlines throughout the day will make sure that you get stuff done leading up to each break or change in activity.

Think about how you work on your last day before going on holiday for a week or two. You snap into ultra-efficient mode. Your drive seems to appear from nowhere. You're a workhorse on a mission to box everything off before you go. Setting yourself mini goals continually throughout the day - *I need to do A, B & C before I leave for the gym* or *X, Y & Z before the Skype call* – has a similar psychological effect. It gives you the spurts of motivation you need to get things done.

Occasionally I deliberately set myself one single goal to achieve in a day – the only thing on my To-Do list. I will then break it down into chunks or mini-goals. By working this way, I can sometimes complete large tasks in a day that have been sitting on my To-Do list for weeks.

Brain Block

How many times have you read the same email 3 times and still not taken the first step in dealing with it? Or repeatedly put off an item on your To-Do list? You just can't get it dealt with. What's that all about? Very frustrating. When this happens, ask yourself these 2 questions:

1. What's stopping me from doing it?

You may not actually know the answer to this. Well you will actually know it, but it may be in your subconscious, not wanting to be accessed at that point in time. The more times you question what's stopping you from doing the task, the more in tune with your brain you'll become and the more aware of it you will become.

2. Can I chunk it down?

It's probably too big or difficult a task. And if it's staring you in the face, it will be overwhelming you and is bound to cause procrastination. You may think I'll just check my emails, I'll just make that phone call, I'll just go and make another cup of coffee. Probably because you just don't know where to start. Breaking it down into bite-size chunks is a very effective way of tackling it.

An example of this would be replacing "Web design for Joe Bloggs" with specific chunks such as:

- Choose 5 images on istock
- Email 1st draft to client for approval
- Confirm which e-newsletter software is to be used (Aweber vs. Mailchimp)
- Embed video from client (saved on client file)
- Do final web amends & email final web design to client
- Invoice client when final approval received

It's basically a project and the project milestones are the chunks.

You can apply 'chunking down' to smaller tasks as well. For example, "Call Ian about rates". This has been knocking around on your To-Do list for a while now. What's stopping you from just picking up the phone to call Ian?

Ask yourself this question for every task that is not getting done. Thinking it through logically and consciously will mean you are able to chunk it down easily. It may be something as simple as you need to run it by someone else first (in which case the next step would be "Speak to John about Ian's rates"). Or it may be that you identify an uncomfortableness with making the call - in which case, it's a frog. Ribbit. Get it on your To-Do list for tomorrow – priority high.

Sometimes you will have to chunk down chunks. It's not important how many layers of chunks relate to one task. The main objective is simply to make an overwhelming task doable.

If one of your To-Do list items said 'Write a business plan' that could be pretty overwhelming. What do you need to do is to break that down. For example, I wrote: "Find Business Plan Template". On day 2, I added a To-Do item "Rough draft of section 1 of Biz Plan", Day 3 "Finish 1st section of Biz Plan, Day 4 "Draft section 2 of biz plan".

Psychologically, these chunks are completely achievable and don't cause overwhelm and procrastination. And in reality, you do more than a chunk at a time – sometimes you get on a roll, and do a little more than planned. That's OK, as long as it doesn't impact on the rest of your focus for the day. So even though you are only doing a little each day, you are likely to do this more quickly overall. This is a real example that I used for myself. I had been putting off writing that business plan for probably over 2 weeks as I didn't know where to start. As soon as I chunked it down, it was done within a week.

Rough Drafts

When you are tackling a daunting task, as well as chunking it down, remember not to be a perfectionist. Start by just banging anything out. Full of mistakes, you're not happy with it – absolutely fine. As long as it doesn't go to a client. That's your 1st draft – the biggest hurdle of your project.

Your next task will be to polish it, to correct mistakes, to pad it our perhaps, to make it into something that you are a lot happier with. If you, like me, are a perfectionist, you will never be happy with it, but you need to accept that. When adding any item to your To-Do list, unless it is truly urgent add it to your list for tomorrow – otherwise it will skew your planning for today.

Keep the Dream Alive

You may want to create a Vision Board (also known as a Dream Board) and put it in a place that is impactful for you personally. For some this is in the bedroom - the last thing you see before you go to bed and the first thing you see when you wake. For others it's the office. It's personal choice, but do what works for you.

A Boost of Inspiration

Create a library of motivational books and keep somewhere to hand. Every time you read a book that you are truly inspired by, highlight the parts that have specifically encouraged you and bookmark those pages by using sticky tabs. If you have a day when you're feeling unmotivated, take 10 minutes out of your day, grab a book from your library at random and read the bookmarked pages to re-energise yourself.

If you like to read books on your Kindle or other e-reader, you can highlight words and paragraphs to go back and re-read.

Mind Mapping

Don't feel like organisation is about writing in neat lines, it's far from this. It's about structure, decision-making and coordinating activities efficiently.

Mind mapping is a liberating way of making notes and capturing your thoughts. My 9 year old daughter had a brain block with a creative piece of writing for her homework. I decided to share with her my love of mind mapping. Very quickly, the content flowed, the stress lifted, and she had glowing feedback on the quality of her finished work. She's used it for all sorts since – planning her new bedroom décor, activities to do in school holidays, birthday celebration planning, etc.

For many years I thought I made the messiest, most random notes ever. I noticed a business colleague looking at my notepad with interest a couple of years ago. *"I know, it's so untidy isn't it?"* I said *"I must learn to write neater notes!"*. *"What do you mean?"* he said. *"It's a mind map"*.

Really? Wow. I had always wondered what mind maps were and I'd been using them all along for years.

Your brain works more naturally with mind maps than lists, so when you're feeling unproductive grab a blank piece of paper and give it a try. You could unlock all sorts of ideas and potential.

Keep your Goals in the Forefront of your Mind

Revisit your goals daily even if you just glance over them. Keep them to hand, where they form part of your organisational folder (see *Set up an Organiser File*, Chapter 2). Or you may want to put them as your screen saver.

Whatever you do, it's important to not lose sight of what you are trying to achieve,

5-a-Day

When you need to tackle a huge non-urgent task, the strategy is simple. You do a little bit each day. But you need to define what that 'little bit' is. And it needs to be realistic. For example, if your task was to clear the backlog in your inbox, you may decide to deal with 5 (old) emails per day. If your task is filing, file 5 items per day.

These small bite-sized chunks won't overwhelm you, but you will feel that the task is in hand. Put a recurring note on your To-Do list with specific actions – e.g. "Action & archive 5 emails today", "File 5 pieces of work today". Simple, easy chunks to deal with.

Always start with the most recent.

Reward Yourself

Reflecting on mini milestones you've achieved and allowing yourself a little treat works well. It helps to keep your focus on completion of a task and provides motivation.

It's important that you establish (even if just in your head) what the reward will be before you start the task. Be strict with yourself and don't allow it until you are finished.

Visualisation Motivates

As it comes to that dip in the afternoon, start to visualize switching off your computer at a reasonable finish time, with an empty inbox, every single item ticked off your To-Do list, no paperwork on your desk and your To-Do list all ready for the morning.

How does that feel? How does it look? Just visualise it and the feeling that comes with it, and use between now and the end of the day to make sure that's what you achieve.

Remove Temptation

Darcy Juarez, Director of Marketing for GKIC (the Glazer-Kennedy Insider's Circle) uses the analogy... *If you're a chocoholic on a diet and you go into a chocolate shop, the temptation is massive. It would be difficult for the most self-disciplined of us not to buy or try the free taster. The answer is simple. Don't go in the chocolate shop.*

If you are trying to focus on getting something done, don't let temptation get in the way. Come out of your emails, don't check social media, switch your phone off. Whatever your temptations are, remove them. The more systems that you can put in place and the more habits that you can get into, the more likely you are going to be to have better self-control. It will be a lot easier, a lot less tempting.

Trick your Mind

Another tip if you are struggling to get motivated is to trick your mind into thinking that you're enjoying the task by identifying the positives.

Treat each Friday as if you are going away on holiday for 2 weeks! And have more holidays. You work twice as hard just before you have time off, so why not take more time off?

J.F.D.I.

I have a J.F.D.I. session at the same time each Friday when I ruthlessly target tasks that I've been procrastinating about or that I'm not sure what to do with. The pressure of only having one hour to actually take action that will add value to my business, is pretty powerful. And entirely achievable.

The rules I set myself for the J.F.D.I. hour are:

- Whatever I do doesn't have to be perfect (this is the most important rule for natural perfectionists like me)
- I can do as little or as many things as I want in that hour (it could just be as little as making a start on one task)
- It must involve some sort of action – which could be simply an email or a phone call to get the ball rolling
- I will not answer the phone, check emails or engage in any distractions during that hour
- I will start promptly at the set time and do no more than an hour

Why a Friday?

It just suits me personally. I didn't randomly select a day of the week. A lot of thought and analysis went into the specific day of the week and the time of that day...

I am mentally preparing for the weekend by Friday. I'm in 'pre-holiday' mode, which means I am on fire! Unstoppable. Excited. Motivated. And more focused than I've been all week. I've just been to the gym (which I do religiously every Friday morning), so I'm fully energized.

When is your time? It's different for everyone. For some people it may be Monday morning when you're feeling refreshed after the weekend. For others it may be a time slot sandwiched between two activities, for example between finishing work and having to pick the children up from school. (see *Setting Mini Deadlines*, Chapter 10).

When are you on fire? If you had to choose just one hour in your whole week when typically you are fully motivated, your decision-making powers alive and kicking, when would that be? When do *you* rock?

Set a timer if you have to, and stick rigidly to it. Don't go over.

Once you've identified your ultimate time, put it in your calendar as a recurring appointment. And stick to it.

And J.F.D.I.

"Simplicity is the final achievement. After one has played a vast quantity of notes and more notes, it is simplicity that emerges as the crowning reward of art"
Frederic Chopin

Summary

Life is so much more complicated than it needs to be. Remember… Simplify, simplify, simplify.

With our hectic lifestyles we face demands left, right and centre, so it's important to take stock on a regular basis. It's all too easy to get carried away dealing with busyness, to plod on in habitual cycles or to fall back into bad habits.

If you are looking to enrich your lifestyle and grow your business then don't just discard this book, or any of the other books I have recommended. Take action! And not just for this week, or this month. Make a commitment to yourself to implement permanent changes that will make your life easier. And if that sounds overwhelming, remember to chunk it down. Eat the elephant one bite at a time. But do eat it.

Combine a little extra discipline of administrative tasks and commitment to invest in new software with a fresh clarity of vision and you have a force to be reckoned with.

Believe me, once you have invested time and energy in implementing changes, both you and your business will reap the rewards. You may feel as you are going along that it's a hard slog, that you're not seeing any results. But I promise you that if you stick with it, it will be so worth it. And it will creep up on you. One day you'll wake up and suddenly realise that your business is virtually running itself; you'll stand back and think 'Wow! When did that happen? *How* did that happen?'

That day is sweet.

Sarah's Recommendations

There are many tools out there to make your life easier and to save you time. Many that I have yet to uncover. In a constant pursuit to make life simpler, I'm discovering more of them all of the time. I would actively encourage and invite you to share your favourite tools with me and I will cover them on my blog.

In the meantime, here is a summary of the tools I have personally recommended in this book – with a few others thrown in – just because. The recommendations would benefit entrepreneurial business owners who are looking to grow both themselves and their businesses.

Books

- First Things First ... Stephen R. Covey
- The 7 Habits of Highly Effective People .... Stephen R. Covey
- Eat That Frog ... Brian Tracy
- The E-Myth Revisited ... Michael E. Gerber
- The 4-Hour Work Week ... Timothy Ferriss
- No B.S. Time Management for Entrepreneurs ... Dan S. Kennedy
- The Millionaire Messenger ... Brendon Burchard
- Figure it Out ... Noel Guilford
- Time Tactics That Work ... Gavin S. Preston

Gurus

- Noel Guilford, The most refreshing Chartered Accountant I have met
- Brigadier (Ret'd) John Thomson OBE QVRM TD DL rcds, Leadership and Performance Management Consultant and all-round inspirational being
- Gavin Preston, Business Strategist, Business Mentor, Author & Speaker
- John Walkley, (Exceptionally perceptive) Business Consultant.
- Brene Brown, Research Professor, Author and Speaker
- Nigel Botterill, Entrepreneur

Systems & Software

- Gmail
- Google Calendar
- Freshbooks
- Clearbooks
- Xero
- Basecamp
- Asana
- Trello
- Mailchimp

- Aweber
- Livedrive
- Dropbox
- Toodledo
- Evernote
- Hootsuite

Hardware

- MacBook Air
- iPhone
- iPad
- Let's face it – anything Apple

Apps

- Dragon Dictate
- ToDo by Appigo
- G-Whizz
- Entrepreneur
- Kindle
- And the Apps for most of the software mentioned above

Stationery Staples

- 5-drawer desktop filing cabinet
- Sectioned, A4 organiser file

- Concertina file

Useful Websites

- www.tpsonline.org.uk
- www.audible.co.uk

If you are interested in knowing where to buy the products mentioned in this book, please contact sarah@sort-it-out.co.uk.

"Life is really simple, but we insist on making it complicated"
Confucius

About the Author

Sarah Rugg is a self-confessed organisation-aholic. Being naturally disorganised made Sarah intrigued to find options to make her days more productive. For years she was on a mission to discover ways to bring more order and simplicity to her life. She discovered many useful tools to assist with the practical implementation. But more importantly she learned how you can re-train your brain to focus only on the essentials. She has successfully applied these organisational methods and now enjoys a more simplistic lifestyle, which has enriched her life.

Sarah runs four businesses, a virtual team of over 25 people and is married with 2 young children. Prior to this she spent 18 years in the corporate finance sector covering a large number of areas, including project management, customer service, marketing and collections.

Sarah is passionate about living life to the full; she works hard and plays hard. Sarah has taken her passion for organisation and turned it into a business. She is a productivity consultant in 2 of her own businesses, and loves sharing her knowledge and learnings to help others to become more productive.